There are only two kinds of videos,
those that earn you income...
and those that don't

Review Request

If you would recommend this book to others,
please consider writing a 5 star review on Amazon.com.

YouTube SEO Ranking Checklists

YouTube SEO Ranking Checklists

Targeted Traffic Using Online Video Marketing

TRACY FOOTE

TracyTrends
New York, USA
KidsandMoneyToday.com

Printed in the United States of America

Published by TracyTrends
http://www.TracyTrends.com
Please send all inquiries to:
TracyTrends
c/o T. Foote
27 West 86 Street, Suite 17B
New York, NY 10024
tracytrends@aol.com

Business & Economics / E-Commerce / Internet Marketing
Computers / Web /Social Networking
ISBN 10: 0-9814737-5-X
ISBN 13: 978-0-9814737-5-8
Library of Congress Control Number: 2013910352

Connect on social networks or comment on our blog at:
http://www.KidsandMoneyToday.com

Contents

Preface

You may find that filming and editing your video seems to be the easy part, so this book focuses on helping you with the promotion and Search Engine Optimization (SEO) or ranking of your videos on YouTube and in search engine results. The book is intended for the beginner through intermediate YouTube channel owner. It is a reference guide of quick tips to increase your sales conversions.

Good videos can be made with fancy high-tech equipment, but they can also be made with smartphones. Because of this, camera and lighting tips are skipped, and the focus is on the optimization and monetization part of your video creation process. The goal is to help rank your videos (be found), bring you traffic, and help you convert this traffic into a source of income.

As a quick-tip reference book, this book is designed for those with some knowledge of the subject matter; you will not find pages upon pages detailing a click-by-click tutorial to complete a task. While you might appreciate this for tasks you are familiar with, you might also feel a little frustration when I cover a foreign subject. But, my guess is you would be even more frustrated if I had ten pages of screenshots that have since become outdated.

Because the Internet changes so quickly, my approach is to tell you, "Complete your profile" rather than "Click here to complete your profile." When you need help beyond this book, I'm confident you could run an Internet search for any topic mentioned, along with words like: tutorial, set-up, help, or the current year, and you will find relevant up-to-date screenshots to finalize any task.

I wanted to share some lists of tasks. You'll find my checklists at the end of the book. There is also a Resource section with helpful links by topic such as graphics, audio, animation, equipment, landing pages, monetization, and organization.

My final thought is to remind you that you do not have to do all of this at once. As entrepreneurs, we have the power to set our schedule, decide our upload frequency, and make our business, our work, fun. I suggest you find a balance between monetizing YouTube and creating video for enjoyment.

~Hope to connect with you over on YouTube,

Tracy Foote

http://www.YouTube.com/KidsandMoneyToday

Why Video?

When you are looking for ways to grab a customer's attention, consider the advantages of using video over print. Video provides additional control, sparks curiosity, prevents theft, provides entertainment, may have less competition, and can save you time by filtering leads to reach a highly targeted audience.

With Internet articles, your customers skim ahead, looking for headers and bullet points to help make a split-second decision to stay or hit the back button. This becomes difficult when you present video. You gain additional time to grab a user's attention. As a business owner, you have more control when marketing with video.

Video also appeals to curiosity. Put a play button on a page and most people will click it. Put a big arrow saying, "Don't click here" and people will probably click at a higher rate. Curiosity is just one step along a customer's purchasing path. You can use video to connect with these customers.

Article text can be scraped (extracted) by software; stolen and repurposed (reprinted, rephrased, or plagiarized) onto another website. You might convert some text to video. Video make is more difficult to steal or copy.

Video can help protect photography and artwork. Internet images are constantly misused or stolen (copyright violations). Four images that you would have displayed on a page can be turned into a simple slide show. It's more difficult to extract an image from a video. It requires more time. Instead of simply right clicking a computer mouse and choosing save or copy, the user must pause the video and capture a screen shot. Video can help deter, but not totally prevent, people from stealing your work.

Some things are easier explained when using video. It can portray a message faster. A step-by-step tutorial article might become an instructional video. The visual explanation can create a more understandable sequence. Would you prefer an article on how to change the oil on your car or a video? Do you reach for the manual on an electronic device or the quick-start diagram?

Video content is fun to share. Videos are entertainment. They are usually short. Because the are visual, they are appealing. When my friend shares a video with me, I want to watch. The emotion I feel upon receipt is a positive one and one of anticipation. When I receive an article link from the same friend, there is a good chance I will bookmark it for reading later. I feel interrupted. Visual is better.

You may find less competition with video. A search for the very general topic of "remarriage" shows 2,460,000 possibilities under the Web results, but 1,390,000 (almost half the competition) in Video results. Check the competition in your own niche.

As an added benefit, Google Inc. owns YouTube, so chances are good that a YouTube video will rank on the first page of Web results. This is in addition to the Video search results area.

Video can boost your credibility. Your viewer will see how many people liked, viewed, or subscribed to a video, and you can use this visual reference to connect with your customers.

Human nature lures us to join groups. Watch a theatre entrance with two windows and everyone's in line for window A, yet window B remains empty. Chances are the next person to arrive will go to the end of line A. The presumption is the majority knows best. Our mind assumes window B is closed or the teller is busy. We tend to go with the majority.

If you can choose a gift behind one of two curtains, and I tell you, two thousand people liked what was behind curtain number one, which curtain would you choose? You can use this psychology in your video marketing. Try to increase the visible cues on your channel such as likes, views, and subscribers.

Videos can also save us time spent with customers. We can use video to screen our customers so we will work with a narrow, extremely targeted audience.

We should aim to mimic realtors who put videos of homes online in order to screen and filter their leads. When their customers call, the realtor knows they have already seen the house. This customer has a higher potential to convert than the customer who may have seen an ad in the local paper.

Keep all these video benefits in mind to create a successful video marketing plan.

Your Marketing Plan

When we think about the fundamentals behind a business plan, we should realize it means making a prediction from an analysis of variables.

We don't say, "Let's throw out some seeds, and see if they will grow." Instead we say, "Our plan is to throw out some seeds and we predict they will grow because we know there is sun, water, and decent soil in this location." It's not until later, that we learn about the rabbit. Then, we decide to make some adjustments to our plan, we make a new prediction, and we await the results.

This is our approach to video marketing. We will spend some time identifying how we can be in the best location to reach a target audience. The goal is to build a plan to rank well, along with a plan to measure and evaluate results, before we even begin to create a video.

This ensures that when you do start to film, you will already know that there is a demand in the market for your product or service. You will already know how to market it, and what results you can reasonably expect when your videos goes live.

Perceptions

When attempting to evaluate successful YouTube channels, your first impressions may not be accurate. With some training, you will be learn to be far more cautious when evaluating the performance of other channels in your niche.

1,535,252
2,519 218

Quick glances can be deceiving. The first thing you might look at is how long the channel or video has been active. Does it have one thousand views in the past day or in the past two years?

If we see a YouTube channel with many subscribers, we may perceive the channel is performing well. And to some extent, this is true. There's no denying that the channel has been successful at collecting subscribers.

If we learn that the subscribers received some sort of freebie or were even paid to subscribe, our perception of the channel may change. This might also give us comfort when looking at our own numbers. Perhaps our subscribers came naturally, with no extra incentive. They subscribed solely out of their desire to connect with us.

We also need to observe the focus of a channel. We might initially look negatively upon a channel with ten subscribers. Upon a closer look, we may find that the channel has a link taking viewers directly to a purchase page, and no emphasis was ever placed on subscribing. How would you judge this channel if you found out it converts 1,000 transactions each month?

We also don't know the usefulness of a channel's subscriber list. How many of the subscribers entered a fake email address? It's a common practice for an Internet user to have a primary and a junk email address. This impacts the true value of a subscriber list. When we view a channel of 10,000 subscribers, what if 7,000 people entered a fake email? Is the channel really a success?

We will also show you how users can subscribe to your channel, yet turn off their notifications. This means they will not be notified by YouTube of your video uploads. This certainly impacts the significance of a huge subscriber list.

Customer incentives, business objectives, and user actions can make it difficult to evaluate the performance of YouTube channels.

Of course you should still try to grow your subscriber list, but all these factors indicate that we can't measure our success or the success of others by the number of subscribers. Perceptions play a role in your business appearance, but a much more important measure of success is sales conversions.

Channel Setup

Even if you've never made a video and never plan to, you may want a YouTube channel as another venue to promote your business.

Three immediate benefits of owning a channel are:

1. *Inbound Website Link:* When you set up your YouTube channel, you can add a link to take the YouTube visitor directly to your website. This gives you an *inbound link* from a credible website. When you have links coming from other website (especially reputable ones such as YouTube) into your business website, this can help your business website rank higher in search results.

2. *Social Credibility*: When you own a YouTube channel, you can display the logo on your website which increases your social credibility. Website visitors like to see logos they recognize. You build their confidence when you display credit card images and social media logos.

3. *Have a Presence*: If someone searches for your company on YouTube, you will be found.

The YouTube channel layout continues to evolve, but you will always have an *About Us*, an image, a description, and so on. The essential concepts to set up your channel remain the same.

Knowing that YouTube frequently moves items and buttons around, we will discuss the general areas, using minimal screenshots. This should provide enough information to get you started in the right direction, and you will have the topic itself, should you need to run an Internet search for a screen-by-screen tutorial.

1. *Channel URL:* You should NOT use your personal name for your YouTube business channel. If needed, create a new channel and watch for the *Click to use a business or other name,* prompt during creation. You may also receive a pop-up, *"Replace your hard-to-read username, and start using the name people know you by."* If you receive this second prompt, Do NOT use your personal name (unless you're someone famous and your name is your brand).

You want to create a vanity (branding) URL made up of words instead of numbers and letters. When working on branding, you might choose your business name for your vanity URL. If you are building a channel around a single product, you might prefer to use keywords for your URL. (You can own multiple channels.)

2. *Banner Image:* Create and upload a banner image that portrays your business vision. YouTube now allows you to upload an image 2560x1440 pixels (large enough to display on a TV). Variations of the middle portion will be shown on computers, tablets, and mobile devices. Display your critical information in the area that appears on *all* devices. This area is shown as the smallest white rectangle box in the image below (1546×423 pixels). Search for *YouTube Channel Art Guidelines* to learn more and download a banner template.[1]

Tip: The lower right corner of the white box area holds your social icons. Busy backgrounds can make these icons difficult to see, especially in Black & White print. (see the next image).

3. *Profile Icon:* Create and add a profile icon. This smaller image will display next to any comment you make on YouTube. Company logos or product images work well. (Make sure it looks clear when shrunk down.)

4. *Privacy Settings:* As with every other social media platform, review and set your privacy settings.

---

1. Google Inc., YouTube.com, YouTube One Channel, *Channel Art,* http://support.google.com/youtube/bin/answer.py?hl=en&answer=2976467

5. *About Page*: Completely fill out your *About* page. Find it quickly by signing in and typing in your browser URL: http://www.YouTube.com/user/yourusername/about, or go to *My Channel* and find the *About* tab, or scroll your cursor over the upper right area of your banner to reveal an "edit" option. Complete all the following entries:

   - *Description:* Complete your channel profile description using your primary keywords in the first sentence; preferably the first words. Your primary keywords are the main words your customer would use to find your business. (Don't worry too much about choosing perfect words when you start. You can revise your keywords at anytime and we will delve more into keywords later.)
   - *Custom Links:* Your first custom link will display on your channel banner as an overlay. You might enter the URL to your blog, a URL directly to your subscription page (for YouTube or your blog), or another link to a specific *Call to Action*. Some text will appear next to this link as shown below.

   - *Social Media Links:* Your header also displays four social media links. You can choose from a drop down list to add: Facebook, Twitter, Google+, Pinterest, Flickr, Tumblr, Instagram, and even more places like Zazzle and CafePress.
   - *Featured Channels*: Featured channels are displayed not only on your *About* page, but also on your *Home* page. As of this publication, they are currently located on the upper right of the *Home* page. Use these for cross promotion of other channels you own, channels of friends you might like to promote, or just a way to highlight your favorite channels.

- *Subscriptions:* Choose to keep your subscriptions public or private by checking the box.

6. *Account Settings*: Found after signing in and typing http://www.YouTube.com/account/ in the URL or clicking *Settings* beneath your profile icon. (Note that this is a different area from *Channel Settings*, discussed next.)

   - *Connected Accounts:* Found at *Account Settings > Connected Accounts*. When starting out, you should probably setup automatic posting of your YouTube activities to Facebook or Twitter. By entering a check in the corresponding box, anytime you upload a video, share a video, click like, or create a playlist, this activity will immediately post to Facebook and/or Twitter. This saves you time and can help increase views, branding exposure, and conversions. Some things to consider are:
     1) *Facebook:* Checking this box connects YouTube to your Facebook *Profile* (as opposed to a Facebook *Business Page*). If for this reason, you do not want to directly connect activity to Facebook, leave this box unchecked.
     2) *Likes:* Clicking *Like* and sharing what you like, does nothing to directly promote your business. The only benefit we can see is that these actions show you are active and kind to others. You might leave this box unchecked.
   - *Privacy:* This is another location where you can choose to keep subscriptions private, but this area also allows you to choose to keep your *Likes* private as well. You can change this anytime. (We discuss the benefits of NOT hiding subscriptions later.)

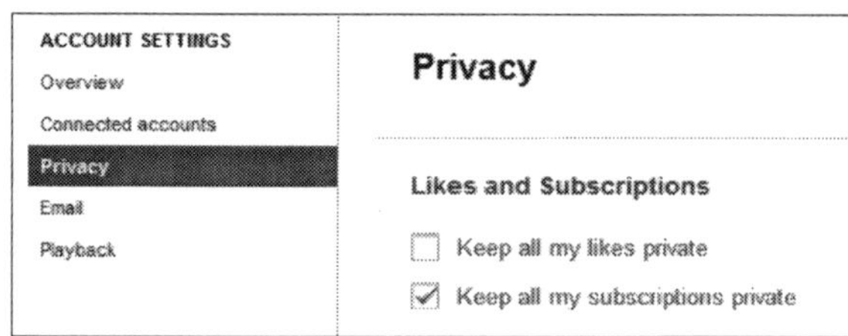

7. *Channel Setting Upload Defaults*: Go to: *Video Manager* > *Dashboard* > *Channel Settings* > *Defaults*. Complete all the items here with special attention to: the initial default setting for your video uploads (private, unlisted, or public) and whether your entire channel will permit comments and video responses.

8. *InVideo Programming*: Go to: *Video Manager* > *Dashboard* > *Channel Settings* > *InVideo Programming*. There are two options that will place a small clickable image as an overlay on *every video* in your channel. The first is your *Profile Image* and the second displays a *Featured Video*. You can implement both at the same time. (Many people choose to turn these off because they can be distracting or the overlay covers some important footage.)

9. *Change Your Country:* The YouTube channel default country is Afghanistan. Enter your correct country by going to: *Video Manager* > *Dashboard* > *Channel Settings* > *Advanced*. You want to have your country correct so you can meet the criteria to enable Monetization.

10. *Enable Monetization:* Follow the steps to activate this. Go to *Channel Settings* > *Monetization*, and click *Enable* or visit: http://www.YouTube.com/account_monetization.

The steps should redirect you to AdSense to link your existing AdSense account or create a new one (if you do not have one yet). Upon completion, you will be redirected back to YouTube.

When you do this, you *Become a YouTube Partner*. YouTube partners join with YouTube to permit display advertising on their channel. You can decide later which videos to monetize, if any. You want to become a YouTube partner to take advantage of the partner exclusive features that might help promote your business (such as custom thumbnail uploads and video scheduling).

11. *Verify Your Associated Website:* After you have enabled monetization, declare your Associated Website by going back to: *Video Manager > Dashboard > Channel Settings > Advanced*. Look for the *Associated Website* option, enter your website URL, and follow the instructions to *Verify*. This lets YouTube know you own the website. When done correctly, your website will be listed with a *Success* button, as shown below:

Associated website

Tell us if your channel is associated with another website. This will help us improve the quality of our search results and verify your channel as the official representation of your brand on YouTube.

http://www. .com Success Remove

12. *Verify Your Account Status:* Become a *Verified Partner* at *Video Manager > Dashboard > Channel Settings > Features*. Click the Verify button and follow the instructions to verify that you are who you claim to be. This is done by a phone call or text message.

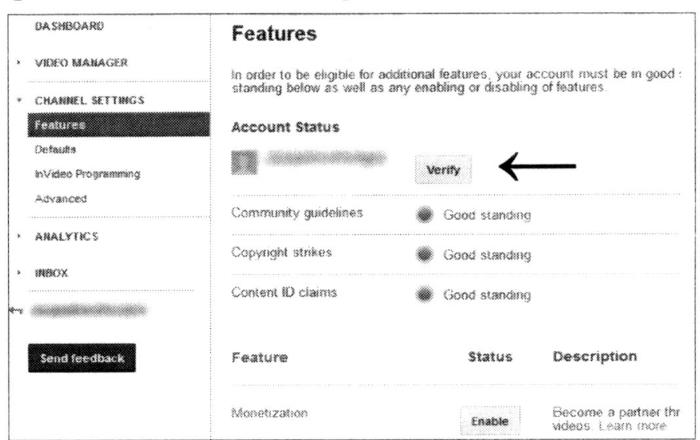

13. *Create a Google Analytics Property ID for Your Website*: Sign up at: http://www.Google.com/analytics to open a Google Analytics account. Create a *Property ID* in the form of "UA-123123-1." This account provides tracking coding that you must add (copy and paste it) into your business website URLs. If you are on WordPress, there are several plugins you might use. With plugins, you usually copy and paste your Property ID into the plugin settings, and it adds the necessary coding into each URL for you.

This coding allows you to begin tracking social hits, clicks to your website from other social media sites (like YouTube). By adding this coding now, you will begin recording relevant data from your website. Let this data collect so the statistics will be there for you to evaluate later.

14. *Create a Google Analytics ID for YouTube:* This follows the same logic as the previous step. You are creating tracking again, but this time, you are tracking your YouTube channel. Create a new *Property ID* in the form of "UA-123123-1" and copy and paste this ID number into your YouTube account at: *Video Manager > Dashboard > Channel Settings > Advanced.*

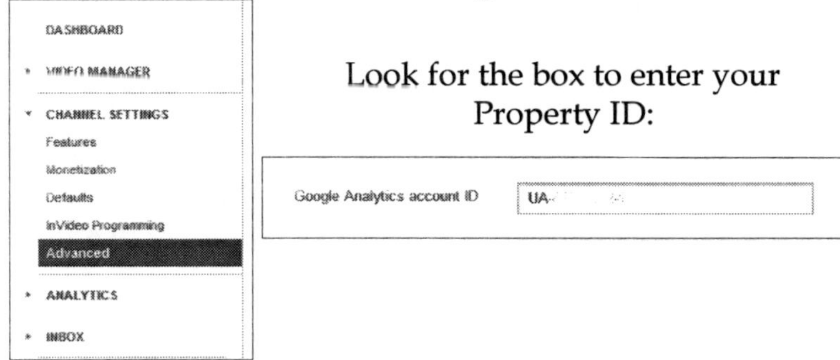

This practice follows Google's recommendation to establish a separate account or separate *Property ID* (as opposed to creating a unique *Profile ID* within the *Property ID* for your website):

> "If you have an existing Google Analytics login, you may create a new account by selecting "Create New Account" in the drop-down on the top right of the page. While it is possible to create a new profile within an existing account by selecting *Add New Profile*, **we recommend creating a new account** so that the data from your YouTube channel does not impact the data summaries from your other websites." [2]

---

2. Google Inc., YouTube.com, YouTube Partner Program Including Monetization, *Google Analytics for Channels*, http://support.Google.com/YouTube/bin/answer.py?hl=en&answer=147619

15. *Link Your YouTube Account to Google AdWords*: AdWords is used when you are ready to pay for Advertising. The reason you want to sign up and link your AdWords is similar to the past two steps. You will begin tracking YouTube visitors that you may wish to target later with a paid advertisement. You can visit http://AdWords.Google.com/ to sign up. Google provides the following instructions:

> "To link a YouTube account to AdWords, create a new online video campaign by navigating to your Campaigns tab and selecting "Online video" from the "+ New campaign" drop-down menu. When you do this, you should see a link to "Link YouTube Accounts" on the bottom left hand side of your screen."[3]

You might also try this path: In AdWords, go to *AdWords > New Campaign > Online Video* which opens up the video sidebar menu. Look for *Shared Library > Link YouTube Accounts* as shown below:

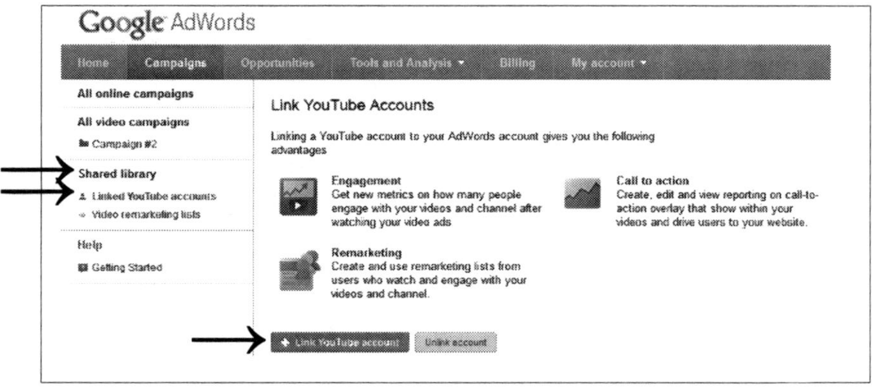

You can also watch YouTube's excellent video tutorial at: http://www.YouTube.com/watch?v=2_-FuDfM6ZM or search on YouTube for the video titled: *AdWords for Video: Linking YouTube Accounts & Building Remarketing Lists.*

---

3. Google Inc., Google.com, *Google Video Ads, Step-by-Step Guide*, http://www.Google.com/ads/video/advertisers/guide.html

16. *Remarketing Lists*: Now that you linked your YouTube account to AdWords, you automatically begin collecting data or lists of channel viewers, channel subscribers, and channel visitors. This is done for you. This is a *Remarketing List* or a list of people you might market to that are grouped by a particular behavior.

You can create additional lists of visitors grouped by specific interactions with your channel. You may track people who:

- Viewed any video on your channel
- Visited your channel
- Viewed a certain video on your channel
- Subscribed to your channel
- Unsubscribed to your channel
- Liked one of your videos
- Commented on one of your videos
- Shared one of your videos

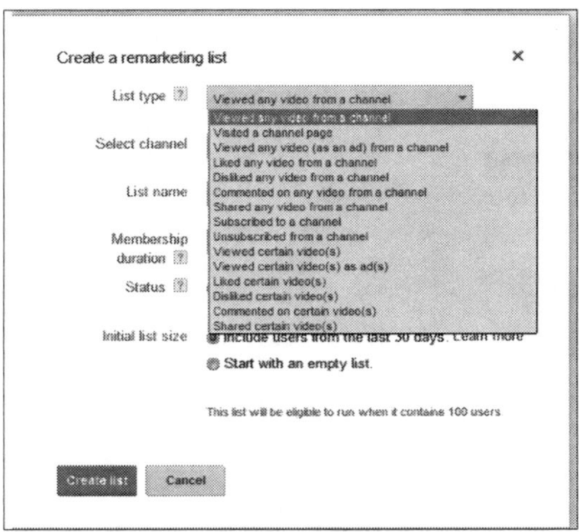

You can keep people on your list for up to 540 days and target them with your AdWords campaign (paid advertising). To learn more, search for the AdWords instructions titled: *Create a video remarketing list.* (After you create a video AdWords campaign, you can find your lists or create new lists at *AdWords > Campaigns > Shared Library > Video Remarketing Lists.)*

17. *Join Google+:* Go to http://plus.google.com/ and set up your Google+ account. In this case, you WILL use your personal name for the account, because Google+ accounts are owned by people, not companies. After you have set up your Google+ *Profile* (for you), you can set up Google+ *Pages* (for your business).

This will not only allow you to gain exposure on another social network (Google+), but it also permits you to participate in *Live Video Calls* (also referred to as Hangouts or YouTube Live) which we will discuss later.

18. *Account Status Check:* If you have completed all the set-up steps correctly, you should have a green button checked on the options shown below on your channel settings.

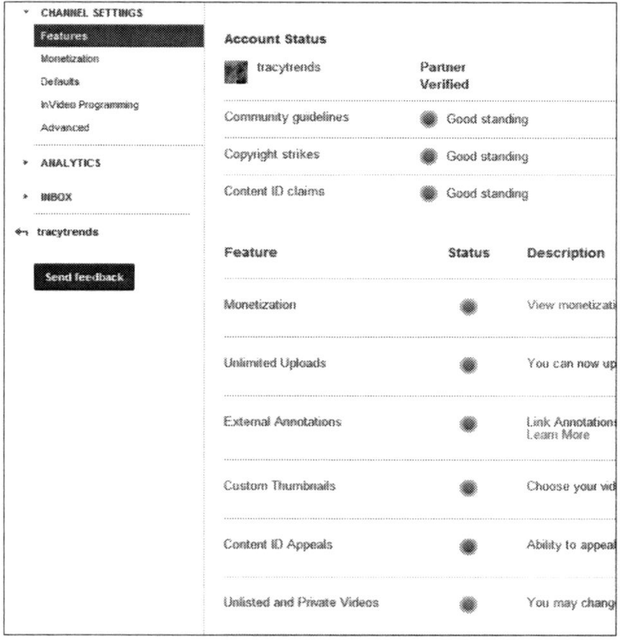

How to Get Started Quickly

Use Playlists

Playlists are a wonderful way to get started on YouTube before you have even created a video. A playlist is a collection of YouTube videos with a similar theme that appears on your channel. These playlists will begin ranking on YouTube and the search engines, which can result in more traffic for you.

Use this strategy to get started quickly. You can generate traffic and interest to your channel and might even gain subscribers without even creating a video.

You can display your Playlists on your channel as several small thumbnails next to one another, checkerboard style, or as a list format with the description to the right (as shown below). Using the list format can give your channel home page the appearance of having significant content. It takes up more space. The casual YouTube user might even think you created these videos.

Playlist (list format): *Military Patriotic Music Songs and Tributes*

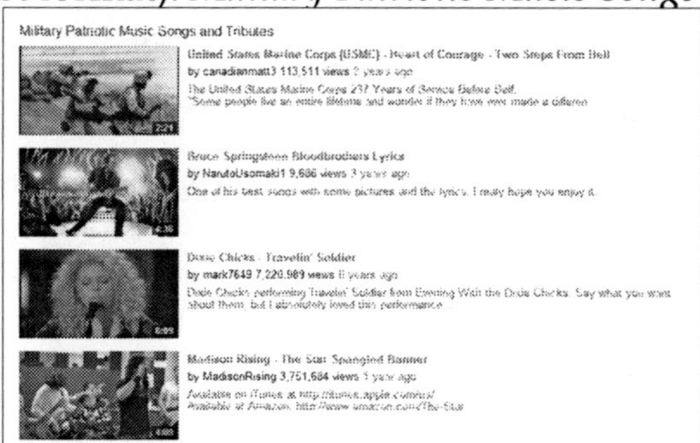

To create a playlist, find a video you want to add, click *Add to* (in the menu beneath the video), and *Add to Playlist* appears.

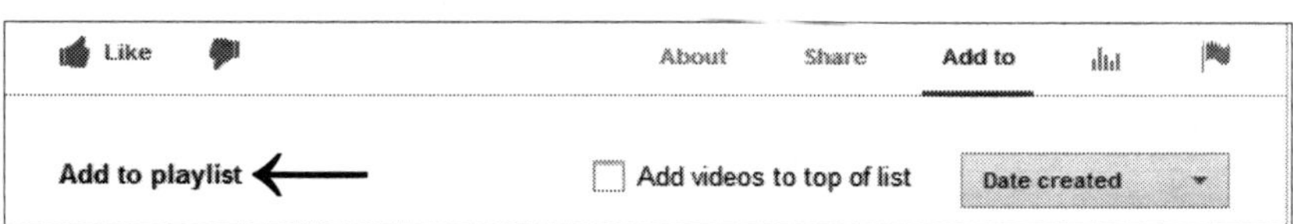

Playlists also rank in the YouTube filtered (advanced) search results. To find the *Filtered Search* option, search for a topic on YouTube and after the results appear, look for a *Filter* button below the search box. (It's a two step process. You can't begin with advanced search.)

YouTube pulls the results of your initial search, and then you can "filter" the results by Upload Date, Result Type, Duration, Features, and Relevance aspects like View Count or Ratings.

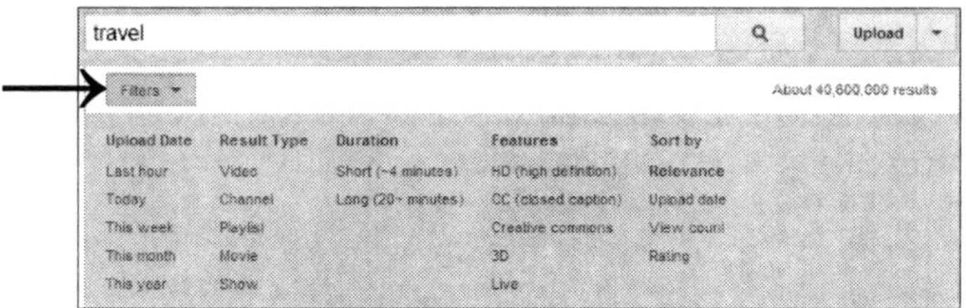

Checklist of ideas to create valuable playlists:

1. Create playlists of categories and topics that are interesting to your target audience.

2. Title the playlists with some of your keywords, keyword phrases, or related interests of your audience.

3. Use keywords in the playlist *Description* and *Tags* to help YouTube evaluate it as relevant for a topic.

4. Share and embed playlists for added exposure and views, which will also help them rank well.

5. Place a link below embedded playlists, asking the viewer to subscribe to your channel, newsletter, or blog.

6. As you create your own videos, add them to your playlists. Playlist additions (how many times your video has been added to a playlist) has been thought to play a role in ranking algorithms.

Playlists can be used for branding exposure, discovery of your product or service, list building, and a strategy to quickly add content to your YouTube channel.

Embedding for Subscribers and Sales

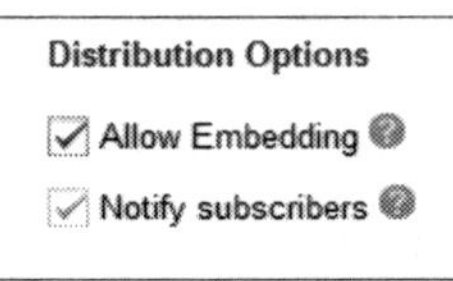

If a channel owner sets the *Distribution Options* to "Allow Embedding" in the video editor (as shown in the image), you will have permission to embed the video.

Embedding other people's videos and your own playlists into you website is a strategic move that can increase subscribers and sales. Embedding is another YouTube feature you can use for conversions before you have ever filmed your own video.

To embed a video or playlist, you will need to copy and paste coding into your website.

- To embed a video: Click *Share* beneath the video and choose *Embed*.
- To embed your own playlist: Go to *My Channel* > *Playlists* > *Playlist Title* > *Share* and choose *Embed*.
- To embed someone else's play list: Copy the coding below and change *playlistID* to the their playlist ID (which you can find in the URL when viewing their playlist):

```
<iframe src="http://www.YouTube.com/embed/videoseries?list=playlistID"
        width="100%" height="500" frameborder="0"></iframe>
```

After you embed the video, you can use it to increase your sales or subscribers. Here's how:

- *For Sales*: Place a URL link directly below the embedded video that clicks through to the product for purchase.
- *For YouTube Subscribers*: You will also place a link below, but this link will go directly to the URL for your YouTube Opt-in subscription confirmation. Link to the URL below and change *username* to your channel name:

http://www.YouTube.com/subscription_center?add_user=*username*

- *For Blog Subscribers*: Do the same as above, but use the URL for your blog Opt-in list.

LeadPlayer

Video players are bits of coding that you place into your website to give you a fancier image or "player" to display your videos. The YouTube embedding code is one example of a video player. Fancier players usually have some special features built in, like sharing or subscribe buttons.

We recommend LeadPlayer which creates a pop-up Opt-in feature within the video. This pop-up will ask the viewer to subscribe (Opt-in) to your blog or mailing list. It can be customized and might look like this:

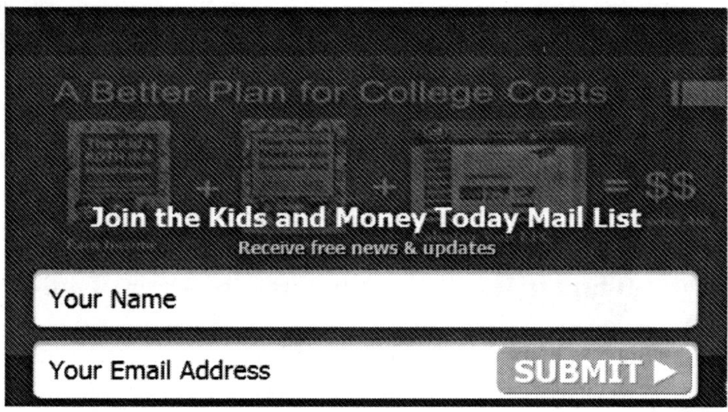

Visist: http://www.kidsandmoneytoday.com/video-player (Our affiliate link to LeadPlayer)

LeadPlayer can be used as a WordPress plugin, but you can also use it on other Content Management Systems (CMS) or use it on a simple html website. LeadPlayer does not subscribe people to your YouTube channel, but instead captures visitor emails into your own mailing list. This means you have direct control of these subscribers. This is a huge, valuable advantage.

When people subscribe on YouTube, they join your YouTube subscriber list—which you do not have control of. You can only see the usernames and channels of your YouTube subscribers, and that's only for the subscribers who choose to make this information public.

The LeadPlayer pop-up can be displayed at any point in the video. If you set the pop-up to occur early in the player, your viewer will have an option to *skip the subscribe offer* and continue watching.

You can embed your own video or someone else's (as long as they have allowed embedding in their *Distribution Options* on YouTube).

That's right. You can use *another* person's video to gain subscribers to YOUR list. This is powerful. You can embed someone else's video review onto your blog, have the pop-up to subscribe display within the video, and the viewer subscribes to YOUR list.

As a strategic move, you might set your subscription pop-up to appear right before the video owner's credits. This can secure the viewer's subscription with you, before he or she sees the creator's closing branding message or closing *Call to Action*.

Embedding of videos is perfectly legal as long as the owner of the video has permitted distribution.

> *Note:* If you do not want people using your channel's videos, leave *Allow Embedding* unchecked in your editor distribution settings.

If you are wondering why channel owners would permit their videos to be embedded, when they know their work might be used in this manner, the answer is: they want the views.

Channel owners are also finding creative ways to protect their branding throughout their videos. A banner placed across the bottom or a logo in a corner, becomes free advertising every time a video is embedded.

LeadPlayer also creates a video site map (this is coding behind the scenes) that helps your videos become indexed by Google Search. (This site map does not always include a thumbnail.)

LeadPlayer's main attraction is its ability to grow your business; potentially grow your contact list, without ever making a video. It should be part of your quick-start plan. Use LeadPlayer for:

- Increasing subscribers to your blog or newsletter list
- Use other people's videos to build your own list
- Site mapping

Find it at affiliate link:
http://www.kidsandmoneytoday.com/video-player

Goals & Conversions

Your Video Marketing Objectives

If your business has more than one niche, you might have to hire someone to help manage your channels or be realistic and choose only a few specific aspects of YouTube to focus on. Videos on YouTube seem to have four common business objectives:

1. Brand Recognition
2. Discovery (help people find your business)
3. Building a list
4. Monetization (either within YouTube or by sending people along a purchasing path)

This is a good time to revisit some questions you might have addressed when you began your business:

- What is your role inside your business and will you still perform this role in ten years?
- Do you expect your definition of your customer today to be the same in the next five or ten years?
- What role will YouTube play in your business ten years from now?
- Are you too passionate about or too close to your business? How will you feel when someone offers to buy you out? Will you be ready to let go?

We're touching on the emotions involved in business so you might ask yourself if the business is *your baby*. Especially if you have been the sole owner, you may find it difficult to make certain decisions. Your decisions may tend to be emotional, instead of being profit based. We want business decisions to be analytical and focused on sales conversions.

Your *Call to Action*

You have to know what your *Call to Action* is in order to know what you wish to rank for. You want to have a clear vision of what a viewer should do, where this person searches, and how you can be listed first in that location.

When brainstorming *Calls to Action*, look to expand each of your business objectives (branding, discovery, list building, and monetization):

- Can you think of ten ways you could connect someone to your brand?
- Are there ten ways people might discover you?
- How can you build your list or are there ten types of lists to entice people to subscribe to?
- Are there ten paths into the different stages of your sales funnel?

Your best *Call to Action* is the one that brings you the most return for the time you invest. Don't overwhelm your viewers. You might decide one *Call to Action* per video is enough. A viewer can only focus on so much in one setting. Test different scenarios. Analytics (discussed later) can help you determine the best location and how many *Calls to Action* to use.

When you are starting out, you might focus on asking viewers to *Share* your video. This has the potential to bring in more views and thus, more traffic. Would you rather I subscribe to your channel or share your information with all of my followers?

Place your *Call to Action* in ALL of these areas:

1. The audio of the video. Tell them out loud what to do.

2. The *Description* of the video. Write you *Call to Action* in the text that appears below the video.

3. The visual of the video. Add a button or image within the footage, the file itself. (This is not an annotation.)

4. The annotations in the video. (Overlay messages)

Annotations

Growing YouTube subscribers is good, growing a blog or newsletter list, that you control, is better. Annotations are speech bubbles, notes (text banners), titles, spotlights, or labels that you can place as an overlay on your video. They can be used to explain your video further, but the sales conversion power is in using them as *clickable links* to complete a purchase or build your list(s).

The annotation setting is located at *Video Manager* > *Uploads* > *Edit* > *Annotations* and appears as a drop-down menu:

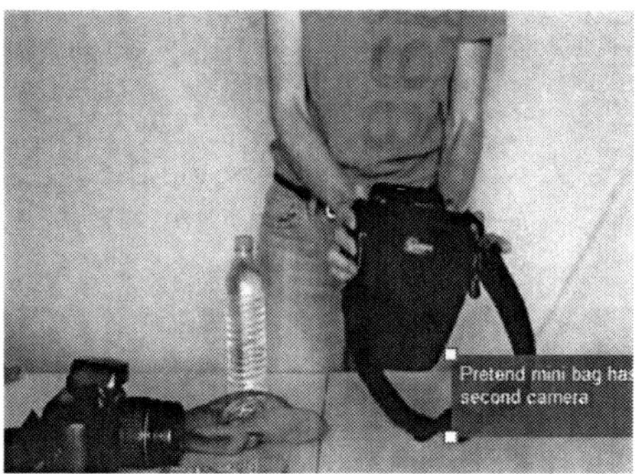

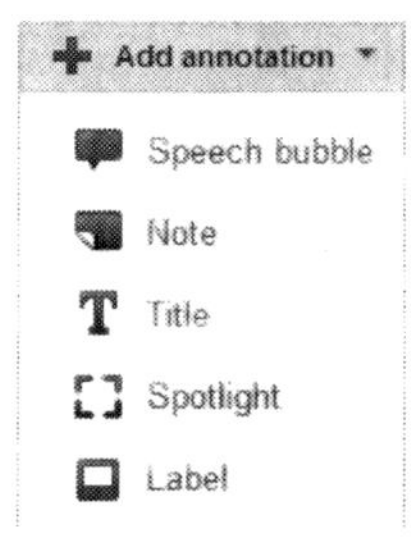

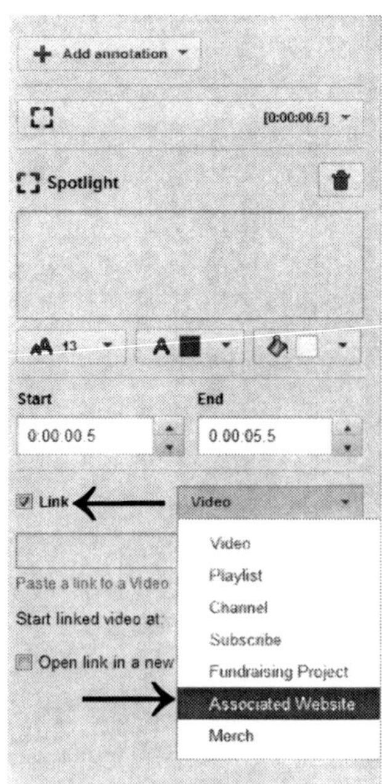

The video above has an annotation overlay on the lower right corner. You can create Annotations anytime after your video is uploaded. This means you can go back to your older videos and add annotations.

Almost all the annotation overlay options can be clickable links. To use your website as the clickable link, you need to be a *Verified Partner* and have declared your *Associated Website*. We covered this in the set-up instructions, so you should show this option as available (as shown in the example image).

The website option appears after you place a checkmark in the Link box and reveal the dropdown menu.

You can use annotations to link older obsolete videos to newer versions. Instead of deleting an obsolete video that still ranks well, create an annotation note, "See the new version. Click here."

YouTube annotations do not appear on all media devices, so don't rely on them for your sole method of conversion. Include a visual *Call to Action* in the video footage and state your *Call to Action* aloud in the audio. This helps users using small devices.

In most cases, you will want to use *Call to Action*s at the end of your videos. Annotations in the middle of your video can:

1. Make your video look more like an advertisement, and

2. Reduce your viewer retention rate (also called "watch time") because the user clicks away and exits before watching your entire video.

A low retention rate impacts your ability to rank well, and if you can't be found, it won't matter how many *Calls to Action* you have, no one will convert.

Ideas for Annotation *Calls to Action*

It might possible to have a one-fits-all *Call to Action,* but you also might consider creating separate videos for your audiences with different levels of experience or expertise. You can direct people from one video to the next or remind them of earlier or lower level videos. This strategy works well with tutorial type videos and helps keep the length of each video short

Consider these *Calls to Action* for your annotations:

- Click "Like" on the video
- Leave a comment on the video
- Share the video
- Subscribe to your YouTube Channel
- Subscribe to your blog or newsletter
- Complete a form
- Sign a petition
- Make a donation
- Make a purchase
- Click through to visit a website

Double Your Calls to Action to Obtain Shares

When your customer completes the first *Call to Action*, you should immediately send a thank-you note and ask or give a reason to share the experience. You might even offer a bonus (such as a coupon or additional PDF file) for doing so.

Implicit Calls to Action

You should include some implicit *Calls to Action* during the editing stage of video creation. These are visual subtle reminders to viewers to do something. You might:

- Include a branding banner (visit your website)
- Show a subscribe button (subscribe)
- Add a product image (make a purchase)

Conversion Rates

We'll discuss measuring and evaluating your analytic reports later, but you want to consider your expectations for your *Calls to Action*. Video marketing is another form of advertising and it's normal for only a small percentage of viewers to convert. Recall that you are probably not reaching your entire subscriber list (due to their notification settings and/or fake email addresses).

If your conversion rate is over ten percent, this seems to fall in the area of doing well. If it is under five percent, that does not necessarily mean you are doing poorly. In some cases, a one percent conversion might be enough for you to live on. Each business and everyone's own personal goals will be unique.

Creating Habits

Video is difficult to convert because users are generally on YouTube for fun or research. We have to break their desire to click another video.

Your *Calls to Action*, combined with your frequency of uploading and interaction with viewers, is all part of a process that creates a habit. You're getting your viewers used to seeing you, used to clicking your videos, and used to sharing. When the offer comes to purchase, they are already used to clicking. It feels natural.

Ideally, their connection should be so deep that they believe they will miss something valuable if they skip a video. This is the ideal emotional behavior or habit of a buying customer.

Your Return on Investment Strategy

Be Evergreen

For the best Return on Investment (ROI), we want to create what is called *Evergreen* videos. Like an evergreen tree, you want your message to stay green throughout every season of the year and for the years to come.

For this reason, you want to avoid placing dates and deadlines within the video footage and audio. It's acceptable to use these in annotations because those can be changed over time.

For example, if you're advertising a 2014 summer fair, you would not use the year in the video footage or audio. You would use 2014 in the video title, description, tags, and annotations. Next year, you simply change these areas from 2014 to 2015. This is much easier than recreating the video. Plus, you retain your history of views, likes, comments, and any traffic you might be receiving from the video embedded on other websites.

Sell the Dream

Your video message is always a promise of change. This is the most important factor to make a sale. What will change for the visitor in making this purchase? In a sense, every sale is the sale of a dream. The customer envisions something getting better as a result of the purchase.

We mentioned that you must rank to have successful *Calls to Action,* but even if you rank, the final sale comes from the content in your video. You need to sell the dream.

This dream is often broken down into *Features* and *Benefits.* The feature is the ingredient, what makes up the product or service. A bike has thick tires. The thick tires are a feature. The benefit is the value to the customer. You can ride this bike on any terrain.

Keep in mind that a visitor searches for information (generally a feature). The visitor searches for "bike with thick tires." But, what the visitor *really wants* is change, a solution to the issue at hand.

Sell the change. Sell the emotion behind your product or service. Apple sells songs in your pocket (not iPods). A video message of, "Enjoy Your Bike on Any Terrain" might convert better than "Our Review of 24" × 3" Super Balloon Bike Tires."

Be Trustworthy

Why should the viewer purchase from you? What makes you a credible authority on this subject?

You can build trust with the "been there, done that" approach. Share your perspective, personal journey, or experience, and tell how your product or service was the solution.

Make sure every video provides valuable content and leaves the viewer more educated than they were before they watched. If you teach them something today for free in your video, they are more likely to trust that your product will also be of benefit.

Offer Value

Let's go back to basic bartering. When there was an exchange of goods, the psychology behind the exchange was that both parties valued the other item more than the item they owned.

Consider the fundamentals in the sale of an item. To make a purchase, your customer:

- Perceives the item as valuable,
- Trusts you to be a credible business,
- Has a need that the item will fulfill, and
- Perceives the value of the item to be greater than the cash exchanged for it

If anything fails along this sequence, the customer will stop watching and leave your path to conversion.

Psychology plays a role in making a sale. The purchase takes place when the customer perceives the exchange to be in their favor. What they will receive is worth more than the money paid. Your video content must demonstrate the value gained by completing your *Call to Action*.

Your video must bring the customer through the emotional stages above. Video is playing a role in your traffic path to a sales conversion.

Extend the Reach of Your Videos

In the interest of Return on Investment (ROI), you want to consider repurposing your video content. This means using the same, rephrased, or slightly altered format of your video to either expand your branding or bring in new audiences.

All your time and effort spent creating one video can flow into varied content across other venues.

Checklist for Repurposing Your Videos

You might use a video as a:

1. *Post:* Embedded video on a blog or guest post
2. *Social Connection:* Post automatically to social sites
3. *Podcast:* Extract the audio from a video, upload it to iTunes, and allow people to subscribe to your podcast
4. *RSS feed:* Create an article or podcast RSS feed (discussed more later)
5. *PDF:* Convert the audio transcript or slide show into a PDF to post on the Internet
6. *Article:* Turn the PDF into an article for a magazine
7. *Reviews:* Turn the PDF into a spin-off article about you, that another author would post
8. *CDs and DVDs:* Sell as a CD or DVD; possibly as a training program or a collection set for a niche audience
9. *Webinar:* Hold a webinar to show the video in segments while you explain the topic further or answer questions
10. *Thank-you Note:* Use a video to thank your customer

Don't worry too much about having your video information in more than one location. In many cases, the person who listens to you on a podcast will not also be following you on Pinterest, Facebook, and other social media networks.

Understand Your Sales Funnel

When we know what we want our viewer to do (our *Calls to Action*), we need to think a little more about our customer. Who exactly is this person that will click? What are they thinking?

If your video marketing doesn't seem to be working, you might take a closer look at exactly who was supposed to find the video., and what term the video was supposed to rank for.

There are many diagram variations of what can be referred to as the business sales funnel. Most include four phases:

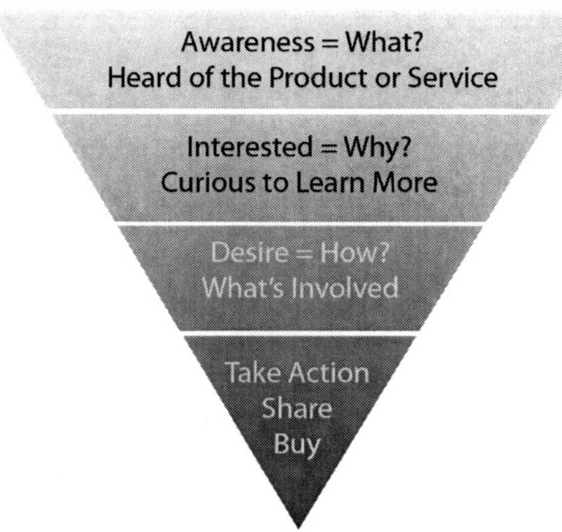

1. *Awareness:* The top of the funnel represents your general audience. These people are aware you exist. They've heard of your product or service.

2. *Interested:* This is a slightly smaller group of people who have already heard about you and are interested or curious to know why your product or service might be important. They want to watch your video.

3. *Desire:* These people understand your product or service is important and want to know how to get it.

4. *Action:* These people are so excited about your product or service, that they share the information or buy now.

Your most expensive customer is in the *Awareness* phase at the top of the funnel. It will take you time to reach these people and educate them about your product or service. Time really does equate to money when you think about whether you want to spend ten minutes with a customer or ten hours if the result wil be the same monetary profit. Your customer in the *Awareness* phase costs you more.

The amount of video shares you receive can help bring customers into this level. Hopefully every time someone shares your video, the top of your funnel becomes wider. The challenge becomes how to efficiently handle these people when they arrive on your channel or watch your video. This will be accomplished in your video content.

Comments can help with the people hovering in the *Interested* phase. These people usually want to see what other people said. They will watch the video, expand the description, and scroll down to read any comments on the page.

Viewers in the *How* phase are your cautious top of the fence or teeter-totter customers. They may be skeptical. Just one small detail might cause them to click away. They're the ones who say, "I was going to purchase until..." and fill in the blank with the price, shipping, personal information required, or some other reason. These visitors have their bathing suits on, ready to jump into the pool. You have to make sure the water temperature doesn't scare them away.

You easiest conversion occurs by connecting to people in the *Take Action* phase. These people may have even purchased a similar solution elsewhere (and it failed). Now, they are looking for a better solution. These people are your best Return On Investment, the highest profit received for time and effort you expend.

You don't necessarily have to bring people through each stage of the funnel, but you should know which stage of the funnel each of your videos is targeting. For each stage, your message needs to say or portray why you are the best (trustworthy) and final (valuable) solution for the issue at hand.

Your Target Audience

We've been emphasizing some essential business marketing concepts. Refreshing these ideas should help you rank and run a successful video marketing campaign. You need to have a crystal clear picture of your business objectives, who your customer is, what they are looking for, and how you propose to solve their problem. If the wrong person is watching your video, then YouTube will serve nothing more than an inbound link playing a small role in ranking your website pages. It will not be a *path* to sales conversions.

We want to use YouTube to:

- Connect with Customers (our *buying* audience)
- Connect with leaders in our niche (our *social* audience)

YouTube is one of many social networks found on the Internet. As such, you need to include YouTube leaders (focused on your niche) as one of your target audiences. These people will be discussed in a later section covering your YouTube community involvement.

If YouTube niche leaders are your social target audience, your customers fall into your buying target audience. To connect with your buyer, keep the stages of your sales funnel in mind and the value of marketing benefits, rather than features. What is your customer thinking and what does your customer need?

Circumstances Trump Demographics

You might separate your buying audiences into your funnel categories. For a weight loss business, the person who has tried weight loss programs would fall into the "Buy Now" category of the funnel. However, actors could be an audience too. They are in the awareness category. Actors are aware there are weight loss programs, but they may not be curious until they are assigned a role requiring them to drop ten pounds. Actors may not meet the demographic traits of your typical customer, but circumstances can bring them straight to the "Buy Now" phase. Circumstances *always* trump demographics.

Filter Your Audience

Checklist of Questions to Identify a Target Audience

Knowledge Level

1. What problem is this person trying to solve?
2. What type of knowledge does your viewer already have?
3. Does your channel have multi-levels of viewers with different expertise, backgrounds, or goals?
4. Does your audience prefer a short series of tutorials or will they sit through an hour presentation?
5. What does your viewer look for in a successful presentation?

Personal Information

6. What is the age, gender, and location of this person?
7. At what time frame of their life is this person trying to solve this issue? (graduation, divorce, new baby, etc.)
8. What types of issues does your viewer connect with on an emotional level?
9. How does your audience find new videos? (search, social media, emails, etc.)
10. What type of video and in what category does your audience watch?
11. What might this viewer need to hear to pursue an idea or complete your *Call to Action*?
12. At what time of day and where will your audience watching the video? Are they alone or surrounded by other co-workers or family members?

Social Interactions

13. What should your viewer hear to inspire them to share, comment, or click Like?

14. What types of videos does your audience share and comment on?

15. Where would your audience share your video and is their extended connection interested in your niche?

16. Who are the people your audience follows, comments on, or subscribes to?

Secondary Audience

17. Do you have a secondary audience, with an indirect interest, who may help convert, persuade, defend, share, or talk about you to your primary audience?

18. Can you find new contacts by researching trends on YouTube?

19. Who is leaving video responses and comments on videos in your niche? Can you interact with these people?

20. Can you connect with other niche or related channels? (On your channel home page, click *Browse Channels* and on individual videos, browse the right margin of *Related Videos*.)

YouTube Community Participation

Leaders in Your Niche

You should connect with the leaders in your niche to build relationships, which might lead to new subscribers and shares.

To find these leaders, you're looking for people who rate, comment, and possibly, upload their own videos. You're looking for the *talkers*. YouTube has already done some research for you. Look at the Related Videos in the right hand column of your video page. Also browse: the *Best of YouTube*, top videos by category, and recommendations at: http://www.YouTube.com/channels. Consider connecting with the people leaving comments on these top videos.

You can review a channel's *Recent Activity* to see how often the owner is uploading, commenting, or adding new videos. Don't evaluate a channel solely by its view count and subscriber list.

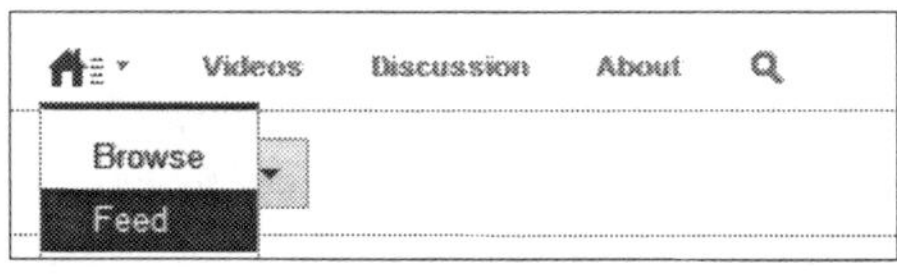

Find the user's activity stream by clicking the channel's *Home* icon (the little house) and choosing *Feed*. Another option is to enter this URL and change *username* to the leader's channel name: http://www.YouTube.com/user/*username*/feed.

Your first challenge with leaders is inspiring them to watch your video. Next, you have to motivate the leader to decide to like, share, comment, or subscribe. Are your videos interesting, unique, and news-worthy enough to share? Leaders don't want their own subscribers to think, "I saw this yesterday."

Subscribe to these niche leaders. This creates a link from their channel to yours which may help boost your rankings. You should aim to subscribe to new channels on at least a monthly, if not weekly or daily, basis.

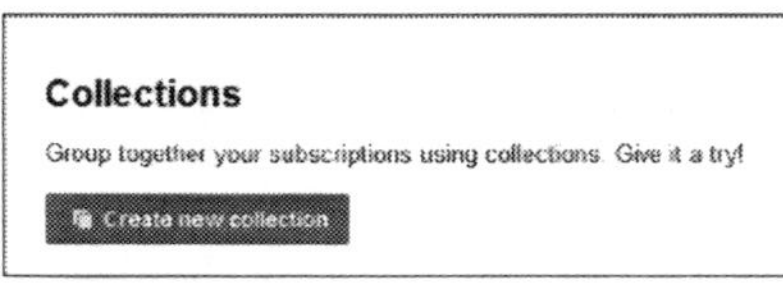

Stay organized by grouping your subscriptions into Collections. Go to *My Channel* > *My Subscriptions* > *Manage Subscriptions* > *Create New Collection* as shown in the image.

Subscribe to Others

Benefits of subscribing to leaders in your niche are:

1. *YouTube Rankings:* When you subscribe to another channel, you create a link and that channel may pass some "relevance" points to your channel. This may help your video rank higher on YouTube search.

2. *Attention and Exposure:* When you subscribe to other channels, you draw the attention of the owner of that channel.

3. *Shares for you:* Once you have the attention of the channel owners, you've increased the chances that they might share your video.

Likes and Subscriptions

☐ Keep all my likes private

☐ Keep all my subscriptions private

We have shown how to set your *Likes* and subscriptions to private in the channel set-up. Since you want to make connections, you might decide to leave this box unchecked. This way you will be visible to the leaders you subscribe to.

If you are adding new subscriptions regularly, you should avoid overloading your email box. Set your email notifications. Go to *My Channel > Subscriptions > Manage Subscriptions* and check the channels you want immediate notifications from. Leave the others blank.

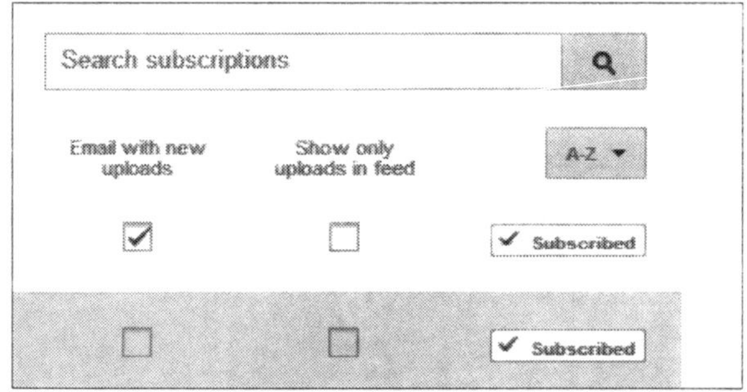

Keep in mind that many of your own subscribers may also have this unchecked, so you may not reach them with each upload.

Your Inbox

YouTube is both a search engine and a social media website. YouTube does very well at keeping visitors watching, sharing, liking, and commenting on videos. It's easy to overlook the somewhat hidden social aspects.

To quickly locate this area: Login to your YouTube account and type: http://YouTube.com/inbox in your browser URL. (There are other ways to arrive here but this is fast and usually reliable.)

Every YouTube account contains these social options:

- Inbox
- Personal Messages
- Shared with You
- Comments
- Contact Notifications
- Video Responses
- Sent
- Address Book

Your Likes

When someone clicks *Like* on your video, the count goes up and this helps your video rank higher in search results.

When you click *Like* on someone else's video, there is no added exposure for you. Your icon does not show on this channel. For this reason, when you choose to participate in the YouTube community, it may be better to say (*Comment*) that you like something rather than clicking *Like*.

Your Comments

When you comment on a video, your profile image, user name, and comment appear beneath a video. This clickable image and username (your business name) can be great exposure for you to get the attention of the channel owner or other YouTube users.

Comments also demonstrate that you are an active YouTube participant. Comment regularly. If you can comment daily, that's probably even better. It should help improve your rankings.

Sharing to Social Media Networks

What's Shareable?

You might make a list of the types of videos you plan to share and what you think makes a video worth sharing. As you make this list, check your own videos to see if they meet your criteria. You want viewers to share your videos.

When you decide to share, remember to stay focused on the interests of your niche audience. You want your shares, comments, likes, and subscribes to raise the relevance of your own channel.

Keep in mind that sharing your own videos can impact the number of "opens" and "click throughs" from your email campaigns and/or blog subscribers. If these people have already seen your video on Facebook, they've no need to open your email campaign, or they may open it but not click through. Stagger your postings and shares so you can use your analytics to see what performs best.

There are a few different ways to post your YouTube videos to social media sites. You will want to run some tests here too, and see which performs best for what you are trying to accomplish. For example: one method of sharing might perform better to increase views, and another method might bring in more subscribers. Let's look at some methods and strategies for sharing.

Automatic Sharing from YouTube

In the channel set-up, we told you how to link your account to automatically share your activity (uploads, playlist additions, likes, or comments) immediately to Twitter or Facebook.

If you set this up, you want to be conscious of every action you take on YouTube. For example, if you have this turned on and you are building playlists, you will be tweeting out all the research you just accomplished at one time, which might seem spammy to your followers.

Also, if you accidentally do something of a personal nature, you might find that you've accidentally tweeted something that doesn't quite match your audience. Your followers will usually be somewhat forgiving if it only happens on occasion, but this is something to watch out for when signed in to YouTube.

Using the YouTube Share Buttons

If you turn off the automatic sharing of activity, you can still share videos in the traditional manner. Every video has a place to click *Share* beneath the video. The sharing options here include:

- Emailing the link to friends,
- Sharing to social media platforms like Google+, Twitter, Facebook, Pinterest, LinkedIn, and so forth,
- Embedding the video on your own blog, and
- Participating in a Video Call (or Google+ Hangout)

When you begin sharing socially, don't forget that you can share a playlist too. This is a great way to gain exposure when you have not yet made many videos.

Share from Your Blog or Website

After uploading your video, you should immediately embed the video into your website. You want to be the first person to embed your video. It helps establish you as the author.

Next, you want to share from your website blog post URL. Use the share buttons you have installed on your website, the ones you entice your visitors to use. When you use these buttons:

1. You view (and evaluate) the same experience your visitor will go through when sharing.

2. You create a direct link from the social network back to your website (as opposed to creating a link from the social network to your YouTube channel).

3. You see how a "share" from this particular URL will appear on the applicable social network. Does it pull the video, image, or worst case... nothing?

4. If your social sharing links include counters, you increase the count displayed on your website or blog.

Alternatively, you can set up automatic sharing using the free Jetpack or other WordPress plugin. You might also use software for auto-scheduling. (See our recommendation at our affiliate link: http://www.kidsandmoneytoday.com/auto-schedule)

Bringing Traffic to Your Website

In many cases, when you post a video URL directly into a social media site, this posts the video and makes the video playable on the site (without forcing the viewer to leave).

A strategy to force the viewer to move to either YouTube or to your website is to post an enticing thumbnail image from your video or a custom thumbnail, along with a link to view the video. Put a comment in the post that says, "Just uploaded my new video, click through to watch." This brings users off the social site and over to YouTube or your website.

A variation of this is to create and use a text image. Instead of a screenshot from your video, use your favorite photo editing software and create an image that is only words. Post that image with the same message. Be sure to only use a few short words so people can read the text at thumbnail size and on different devices.

Pinterest

When you embed your video onto your website, you want to include a 200×200px image inside the article text, somewhere beneath your embedded video. This creates an image that can be picked up by people who wish to pin to Pinterest.

You can follow the previous idea of using an image clipped from within your video, or you can create a text or other image with some sort of *Call to Action*.

You should also share to Pinterest yourself. You can create a separate Board on Pinterest for all your videos. Title the Board with your main topic and the word "video." As you create more videos, create new boards grouped by topic.

Each of your Pin descriptions on Pinterest should include:

- An enticing title that includes keywords
- A description sentence using your keywords,
- The keyword "video" to help your pin rank well, and
- The target URL either to: your website article/post, your YouTube channel, or direct to your YouTube Opt-in confirmation URL (shown below).

http://www.YouTube.com/subscription_center?add_user=*username*

Schedule Multiple Shares on Facebook

You can go to Facebook and use their schedule posting feature to schedule your video once a quarter over the next year. (After that, you might come back and reschedule it out every six months.)

You might post with the opening, "Have you already seen my video on..." and add the topic of your video.

This scheduling will allow you to pick up some new views from people who became fans after your initial upload or from people who missed your original shares.

To schedule a Facebook post, you click the little clock icon beneath the status window and choose the year, month, date, and time you want your post to appear.

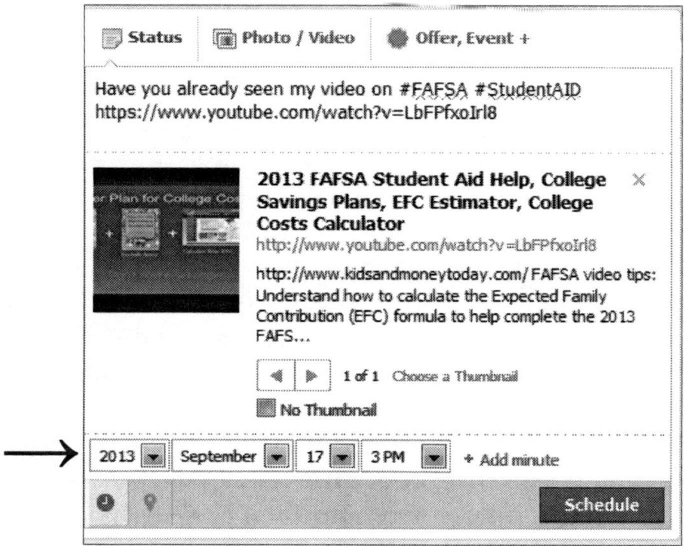

Staying on Social Media Networks

There are social advantages to letting users watch your video on a social media site, so occasionally, do this too. Benefits include:

- Additional video views
- Increased personal activity on the social site, which is good for credibility, branding, and social interaction
- Increased visitor interaction on the social site through shares, likes, comments, and perhaps new followers

YouTube and Google Search

The simple rule to ranking is: be relevant. Everything we've addressed thus far contributes to the relevancy of your video. You have tips to:

- Evaluate your performance (as opposed to perceptions)
- Establish a channel that clearly indicates your niche
- Collect subscribers without even making a video
- Create *Calls to Action* related to your topic
- Know the need your niche audience searches for
- Participate in your niche within the community
- Share to social networks to increase channel activity

All of these play an indirect role in establishing your expertise, authority, and relevancy which will improve your ranking in the search results—for your targeted customer, the one ready to purchase within your niche.

Another strategy that may help you rank higher is to consider restricting all your Internet browser actions to areas within your niche. This means when you are working on your business, you sign into all your social accounts (Google+, Twitter, Facebook, Pinterest, YouTube and so on). Since Google tracks your movements, the idea is to connect all your activity together under one umbrella of expertise. You can even set your browser to launch these windows upon opening and then close each window after you have done at least one interaction for the day. (If you have more than one niche, either sign out and sign in again to the new niche site, or use different browsers.)

This practice may also help you discover new areas you might share with your audience. You may also find new competitors. You should begin to see more ads and search results related to your niche. This happens because competitors are targeting you with their own remarketing programs. (You may recall that a remarketing program displays interest based ads to you based on sites you have visited and actions you have taken on the Internet.)

Site Maps and Rich Snippets

To see if videos on your website are being indexed by Google, enter: site://www.*yoursitename*.com into the Google Search box, change *yoursitename* to your actual website, click the *More* tab, and choose videos.

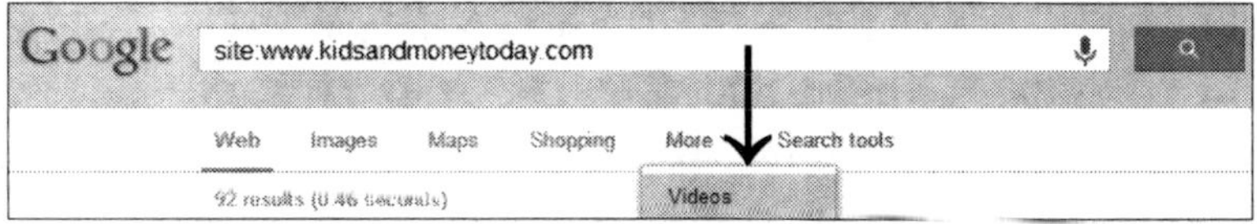

If you have no listings in the results, then your videos from *your website* are not yet indexed.

Ideally, you want your website videos indexed on Google with Rich Snippets and a thumbnail. This means when viewed in the search results, the appearance would look like this:

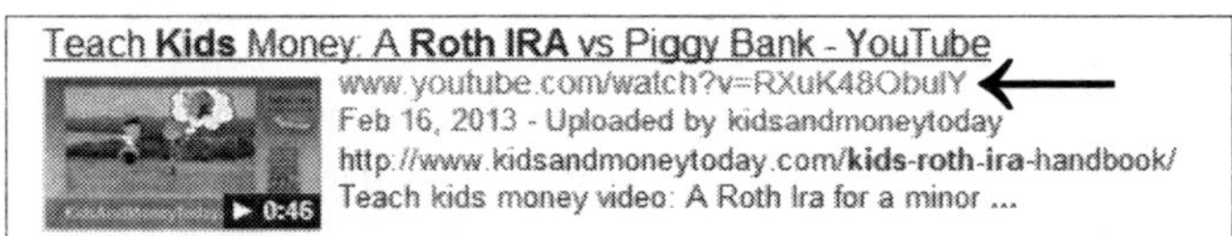

Notice the Rich Snippet above is for a video listing located on YouTube. We mentioned earlier that LeadPlayer can help create a Video Site Map for videos embedded on *your website*. LeadPlayer does index your videos, but Google Search results do not always display a thumbnail with the coding.

Good Habits for Kids Video: Roth IRA vs a Piggy Bank - Kids and Mone...
www.kidsandmoneytoday.com › child roth IRA
Good Habits for Kids Video: Cartoon video teaches a money lesson. Two working children discuss where they are saving their earned income.

The above snippet is from the same video, but in this case, the video is embedded on the business website, in an article using LeadPlayer. Which listing do you find more enticing to click? (The main benefit of LeadPlayer is the Opt-in feature, not site maps.)

Suffice it to say, we would like all our videos to appear in both Google Web search and Google Video search in the Rich Snippet format with a great thumbnail.

Video site maps is an advanced subject, generally beyond the scope of this book, but at a minimum, you can see what your goal should be for appearance, when ranking in search results.

Rank for Your Keywords

We discussed identifying your customers need so you can connect with their emotions involved in making a purchase. You still have to figure out exactly how your target audience searches for solutions. This is the role of keywords.

Keywords are the words users type in a search box to find something they are looking for. These are the words you will place as *Tags* in your video to let YouTube know you are a relevant video to show in search results. They are the words you want to rank for.

A good ranking strategy is to limit your video focus to one idea. This means one keyword or a short keyword phrase per video. This approach narrows down YouTube's choices for ranking.

Suppose you have three videos on tourist information for New York. You might focus one video on the keyword phrase "New York travel," another on "New York trip," and the third on "New York vacation."

A common mistake is to add these phrases to all three videos. If you did this, it would be like placing all three videos in a hat and asking YouTube to pick one for "New York trip." All three videos would be competing against each other with a one in three chance of being selected for spot number one.

A better strategy is to avoid duplication and have a unique focus for each video. You are simulating being the one video in the hat when YouTube (or Google Search) pulls a result. You say, "No need to guess. This is the video I want you to rank for this term."

Of course, this practices only eliminates competing against yourself. You still have to beat out the competitors for that number one position.

Aside from saying, "This is MY best video on the topic," you want to indicate that your video is more relevant than any others for these targeted keywords. You've already established a good start by indicating your channel belongs in this niche and you are socially active within this niche.

But, before you can rank for your keywords, you have to identify them. What are the best keywords that will pull in the desired amount of targeted traffic (because they have a high number of users searching for them), and also, words that you have a good chance of ranking for in the top position of the search results?

You want to look for keywords with a high number of searches. Searches transition into traffic, and with more traffic, you should have more conversion opportunities. Make a list of keywords and long-tail keywords (your keyword plus a few more related keywords).

Checklist for Keyword Research

1. *Brainstorming:* Review your target audience list and make a list of keywords you think they might enter.

2. *YouTube Search Box*: Start typing your keywords into the YouTube search box and see what suggestions YouTube automatically creates as you type.

3. *Google AdWords Keyword Tool*: Use the *Phrase Search* at http://www.AdWords.Google.com/o/KeywordTool and choose a keyword(s) with at least 10,000 monthly searches. (Don't worry about the competition column.)

4. *Call-to-Action Words*: Make a list related to your *Calls to Action*. Your keyword phrases might include words like: purchase, buy, how to, help, tutorial, and so forth.

5. *Frequently Asked Questions (FAQs)*: Make a list of keywords associated with the question most frequently asked by your customer.

6. *Trend Observation:* What type of videos are currently ranking? What are the leaders in your niche focused on? What do your subscribers comment on? What products are popular on Amazon.com right now and what are people discussing in Amazon.com reviews? Check this same type of information on Google+, Facebook, Twitter search, Yahoo Answers, niche forums, Pinterest, Yelp, and other social networks.

7. *Analytics:* Use your analytic reports (discussed later) to see the exact phrases your viewers used to find your video. If you do not have a video already targeting these keywords, you might create one.

Evaluate Your Competition

It's easier to rank within YouTube results, than Google Search. This is because there is less competition. The second easiest place to rank well is the Video tab of Google Search. Here you have competition from YouTube plus video hosting sites and individual websites hosting their own videos. The main Google Search is most difficult because your video competes against articles plus videos for position.

Place your keywords in a column in a spreadsheet. Go back to YouTube. Type your keyword into the YouTube search box and record the number of videos that currently exist for that keyword. This number is currently located beneath the *Upload* button.

Sample search for *New York vacation*

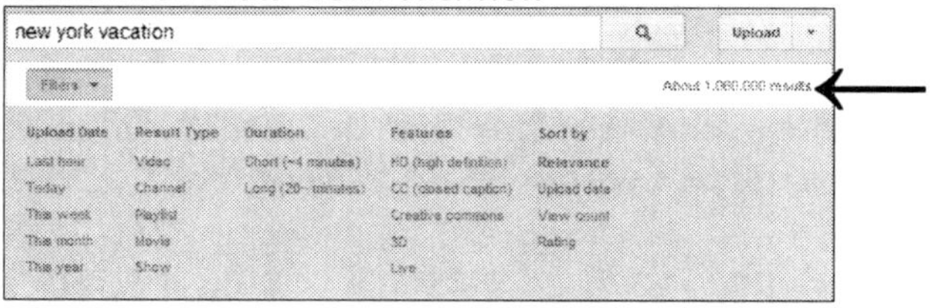

In the image above, there are 1,060,000 other videos with some sort of relevance to *New York vacation*. This is your general competition on YouTube. This is the competition you should be most concerned with. This is more important than the competition numbers displayed in the AdWords tool, because AdWords is measuring the competition in Google Search.

Add a column in your spreadsheet titled Number of Views. Record the number of views that the top ranking video has. Videos will fluctuate in their positions. This is to give you a general feel concerning the keyword.

A spreadsheet might look like this:

Keyword	# of Searches	# Videos on YouTube	Number views for top video
A	10,000	1,060,000	65,754
B	12,000	1,000	200
C	40,000	9,000	5,000

You can use your spreadsheet to:

- Decide which keywords to focus on first
- Develop a realistic expectation of how soon you might rank in the top positions on YouTube
- Predict the number of views your video might receive (by reviewing the current top ranking videos)
- Predict the potential traffic your video might generate

Long-tail Keyword Ideas

As you research your keywords, consider the impact of small add-ons. A group of keywords is referred to as long-tail keywords. Examples might be things like buying keywords, local keywords, informational keywords (targeting people who are in the learning phase of your buying funnel), emotional and inspirational keywords.

Emotional keywords can help with conversions. Do you want party favors or fun party favors? You will have to do some testing to see which keyword variations perform best.

Don't forget to include words related to self-improvement or tutorials. These are popular areas for YouTube users.

Try using these words as additions:

- video or online video,
- year (the current year),
- location (your city, town, and/or state),
- buy, purchase, or for sale,
- review
- how to, help, information, or tutorial,
- playlist.

Multiple Videos with Similar Keywords

It's a good idea to create multiple videos with similar keyword variations. This can help portray your channel as an authority on a subject, and this should help improve your rankings.

In our previous example, if we made three videos: New York travel, New York trip, and New York vacation, we are beginning to set our channel up as an expert on visiting New York.

Video Page Optimization

When you know who your audience is, what they are looking for, and how they are looking for it (keywords), the next step is to be sure your target audience can find you. This means ranking in both the Google Search engine and on YouTube for the keywords your customer is typing.

The basic concepts to rank well apply to both YouTube and Google Search results. These factors will help indicate that your video is relevant.

Title

Begin your title with your keyword phrase. Try to have the most important keyword come first. The first word is thought to count the most for ranking, then the second, then the third, in a sort of weighed algorithm. Keep your title short. You should find your long-tail keywords will rank faster than shorter keywords.

Description

YouTube descriptions tend to be full sentences as opposed to bullet or outline format. Begin your description with the primary URL where you would like the user to visit next. This is usually the URL for your *Call to Action*. It could be a purchase page, a page to subscribe to your blog, a page to download a free item, or another path you want your visitor to take.

To create a clickable link, you must use the full URL, including the http:// part of the address.

By placing this link first in your description, the link will be visible in the snippet description that appears on YouTube search results. This means the URL is visible before the viewer even chooses to click on your video. This visibility may help gain interest and encourage clicks.

Description in YouTube search results:

When the user clicks to watch, the link will, of course, appear on the video page itself. But by placing it first, you also have an additional exposure on the search results page.

Descriptions on the individual video pages are collapsed. Users have to click *Show More* to view a full description. By listing the URL first, the link is visible as the user watches your video. Curious and interested people (in the middle of your sales funnel) will want to click to see where the link goes.

Description shown on the video page:

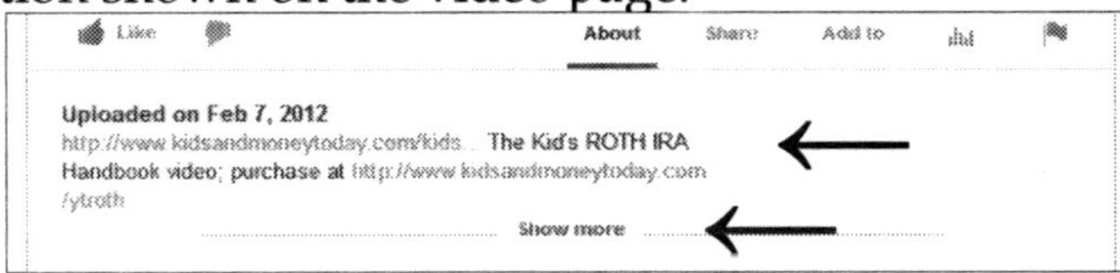

You will see some channels use a sandwich approach. This means you immediately begin your video description with your URL, add a keyword sentence, and then place the same or a similar URL after the sentence. We use this approach.

When your video is live, always test your link by clicking it. Typing errors are easy to make and will kill your conversions.

There are mixed opinions on how long your description should be, but most channels include a few short sentences. Others add two paragraphs. A popular conversion strategy is to use teasers with links for "more information" or "read the rest on the blog."

Many descriptions are now including social links to connections like Facebook, Twitter, Google+, and Pinterest. The idea is that if viewers missed your *Call to Action*, but took the time to expand the description, they might be interested or curious enough to connect on other social sites.

Since description URLs are listed with the http (not coded with anchor text), it's helpful to precede each link with an explanation. The most common method of doing this is to use a *Call to Action* phrase or all capital letters as in these two examples:

Like me on Facebook:
http://www.facebook.com/username

TWITTER
http://www.twitter.com/username

Category

Choose the most relevant category for your video. If it fits in two categories, do some research to see which category has more activity on YouTube and begin with that one.

Later, you might test to see if another category performs better. The category with the most activity, may not be the one that has the highest conversion rate for you.

Location

If you are a local business, it may help to state the location of your business. If you are solely an online business, you might use the location to show where the video was filmed, especially if it is a travel video.

Tags

Tags should help your ranking position in YouTube search results, and *Tags* may also let Google know what ads to place as overlays and on the side of your video page. This is important if you choose to monetize your videos by running ads on them.

Use your keywords, related words, and/or long-tail keywords to create about 10-15 tags for your video. Tags are separated with commas. A phrase would be two words together. For example, in a Peru video, you might have: Peru, video, Lake Titicaca, Titicaca, and so on. Do not list the tags as: Peru, video, lake, Titicaca. The word "lake" is not a desired or relevant keyword.

Did we need to list Titicaca twice? Only Google Inc. can be one hundred percent sure if you need both. If we want to rank for the term "Lake Titicaca," it's safe to assume we should begin testing using it as a phrase positioned at the beginning of our tag list.

If we are trying to rank for long-tail keywords, the separate listing of Titicaca might pull our video into keyword results for a combination of words that we had not yet thought of. We can use our analytics to discover these new words and phrases and possibly use them for new videos.

You should test to see how tags impact your search results and conversion.

Tags also can help with related videos. Your second tag of every video should be a unique uncommon term that no one will search for. Let's give this *Tag* an unofficial name and call it your *Channel Tag*. This *Tag* could be a phrase or a mixture of numbers and letters (password format). A phrase is preferred because it could help with long-tail opportunities. It just needs to be something very unique that would not normally be entered as a tag.

Your *Channel Tag* connects all YOUR videos together as a related group. This helps pull your channel videos (as opposed to other people's videos) into YouTube's sidebar display.

Tags can assist with related videos. The image below is a screenshot from one of my Peru videos. You can see in the right sidebar, YouTube has pulled three other videos from MY channel to display. As I create more videos, I could potentially take over the entire right sidebar, which will help with branding and should increase the views.

This illustrates how you can use a *Channel Tag* to try and eliminate competitor videos from displaying.

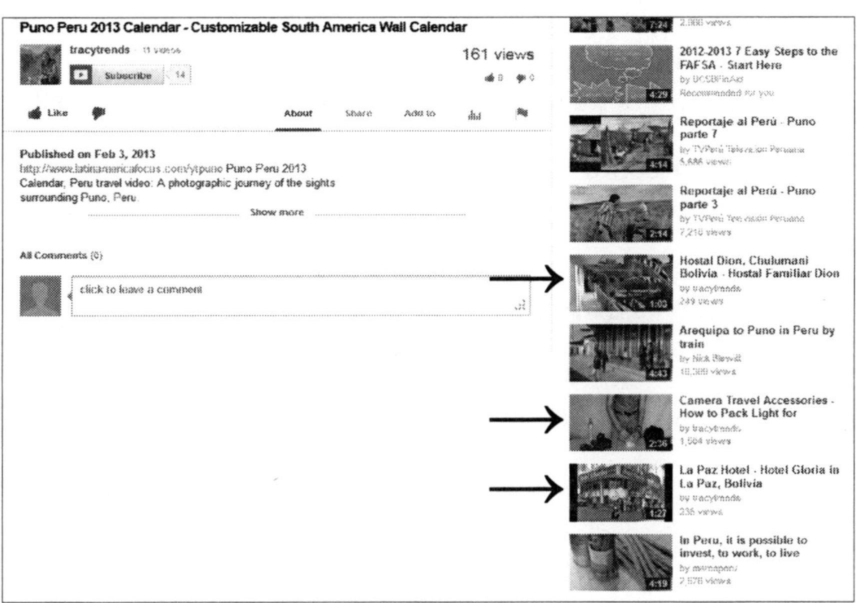

Playlists

After uploading your video, immediately add it to one of your indexed playlists or create a new playlist. Playlist additions may factor into ranking algorithms, they show up in search results, and they are another opportunity to gain some additional views.

Transcript and Caption Files

We discussed how *Title, Description,* and *Tags* help indicate that your video is relevant for a search term. You can send another signal by using transcripts.

With transcripts, you turn every word used in your audio into text to that can be read by Google and YouTube. Because of this, you should plan to include keywords and a verbal *Call to Action* in the audio of every video you create. This includes your videos and slideshows with instrumentals (music without words). You need to include some sort of audio *Call to Action* in the introduction and closure so you can create some text for a transcript.

Transcripts are also useful if you plan to post only the embedded video as a blog post. You might copy and paste the full transcript to appear directly below the video. By adding the transcript, you provide content for spiders to crawl which helps your website page rank higher in search results.

The transcript and caption options are found in your video editor under the *Captions* tab. A caption file is a transcript file with time codes. Caption files are written as a text file in this format:

0:00:08.360,0:00:10.030
My beginning text would be here.

0:00:11.219,0:00:14.349
This is text that begins at about 11 seconds into the video.

0:00:14.349,0:00:16.869
This text starts 14.349 seconds and lasts until 16.869 seconds.

The easiest way to add a transcript file is to upload your video and wait for YouTube to create a caption file. This might take a few hours, but YouTube does this for you automatically.

The file accuracy will depend on how well the YouTube text-to-speech software recognizes the pronunciation used within your audio file. Most likely, you will need to make corrections.

In the next image, we can see the generated transcript is a jumbled mess. It has guessed at the word "caterer" and uses incorrect words and grammar such as: "and that they inspects."

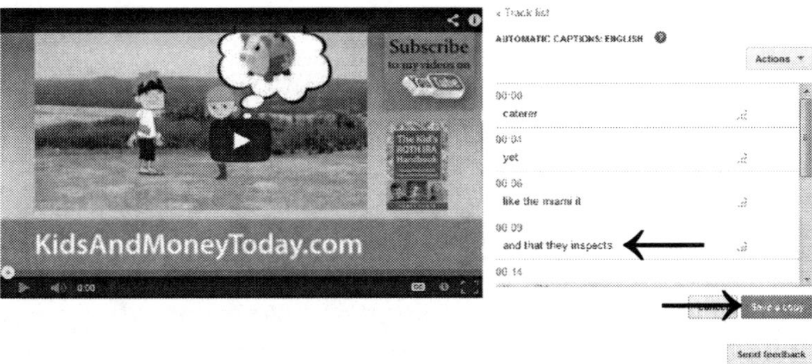

To correct your file, click *Save a Copy* and download the caption file. This will be a .txt format file. You can edit this in your favorite editor (such as WordPad), and save it as a .txt file. Then, go back to your YouTube video editor, click *Add a New Track > Upload Caption File or Transcript* and add the corrected file.

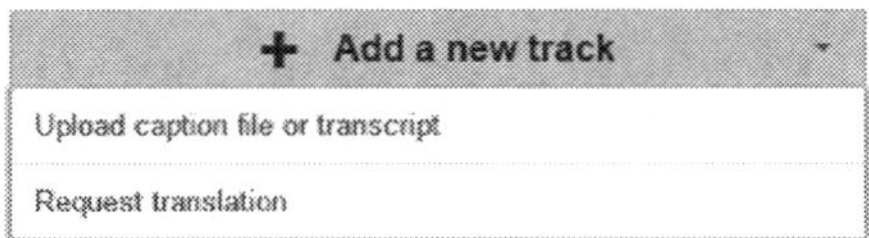

The transcript should appear correctly now (as shown in the image below). Click the tiny cc button on the lower right of your player to view the captions within your video. Watch the video and review (read) your caption transcript as the video plays. Check that the text flow is in synch with the audio. In some cases you may need to re-edit the time codes to have them line up with the audio voice. (Just make the correction and re-upload.)

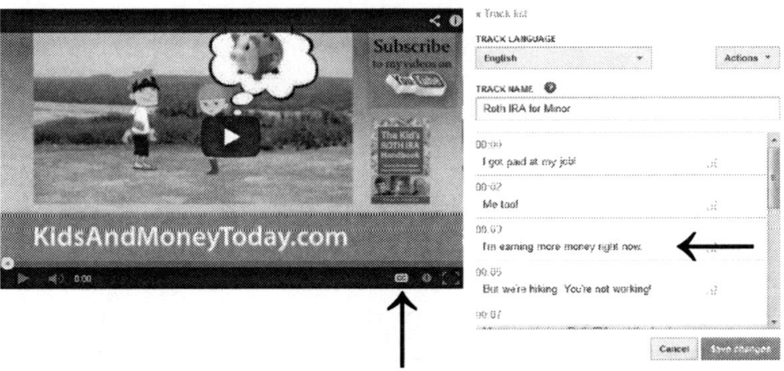

Other Ranking Factors

Age and Freshness of Video

The age of your video plays a role in ranking. When you first upload a video, it has a high level of *freshness*. It's brand new. Google and YouTube love new content, so we get some *kudos* points, and we rank higher while our video is considered new.

Ironically, you can also get some *kudos* points for being old. If you've been doing something for a long time, you are viewed as having experience and credibility. Website domains established since 1999 are valued for their *age*. This age factor can nudge them higher in rankings.

This is one reason to get your channel started early, even if you are not yet making videos. The channel will grow and so will its age (when it was established) and this may help your rankings.

Another concept regarding the term "age" is *premier*. It helps to be the first video on a subject. Google Search will usually rank the original posting of content higher than any duplicate posting. You should aim to create the first tutorial, first review, or first to break the news on something. This should give you a nudge forward to rank above later videos. Try to be the first on a topic.

What weighs more freshness or age? Suppose there are already six videos on a topic, and you post a new one (number seven). Initially, you will probably get a freshness boost and may outrank some of the others (because you are new). But, you are also duplicate content. The initial (oldest) posting may still outrank you. As all seven videos become "old," the other ranking factors (views, watch time, etc.) will kick in, and positions will shift. To hold a position, you need to do more than post fresh content.

Consistency

All activity on YouTube is a good thing. From uploads to comments to shares, you are indicating that you are an active channel. Consistent upload activity is even better.

Everyone has their own creative block when it comes to video marketing. Some can't come up with an idea, some are afraid of the camera or don't like the sound of their voice, and for others, the entire process seems too time consuming.

The different sections of this book, along with the Resources in the back, should help address most of these concerns.

Schedule Your Uploads

If you are a *YouTube Partner*, which you should be if you applied (in channel set-up) and were approved for monetization, you will have the capability to schedule your uploads. This can help you establish consistency.

You schedule your uploads in the *initial step* of uploading a video, *before* you choose your file to upload. Click on the Privacy dropdown menu (as shown in the image below) to choose *Scheduled* and follow the steps.

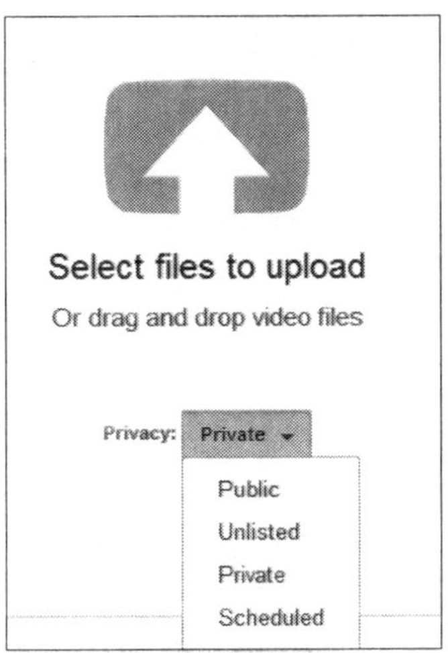

One strategy for consistency is to create 12 videos and schedule them for one per month. Then, make 12 more videos and begin scheduling them at 6 months out, so now you will have two videos per month beginning on month number six. Make 12 more videos and schedule them 9 months out and so on. This way you slowly work up to one video per week and have a steady schedule going. This also gives you time to work on high quality videos, and more importantly, time to take a vacation. Entrepreneurs who use scheduling can actually be on the beach, traveling, or hiking while their business is on auto-pilot.

Embedded Videos Impact Rankings

When your video is embedded, this will increase views, which boosts ranking. The quality and relevancy of the site where your video is embedded will also factor into rankings.

It makes sense that you would want your video embedded on a site within your niche, and it makes sense that the more niche embeds you have, the more relevant you will be.

Inbound Links to Your Channel (Backlinks)

Inbound links are another indication of relevancy. You want links to both your YouTube channel and each video URL. To create inbound links:

1. Promote your channel URL as a link on your website.
2. Embed your videos in several locations on your site.
3. Below your embedded videos on your website, place a text link to the video URL on YouTube.
4. Share your channel URL and video URLs to social media.
5. Ask viewers to share your videos.
6. Subscribe to niche channels on YouTube

Viewer Retention Score - Watch Time

Your audience retention score refers to how well your visitors engage with your video; the percentage of the video watched. YouTube places greater emphasis on *Watch Time* than views, so use analytics to see where viewers drop off. To increase or maintain your viewer retention:

- Don't have any monotones or dead time
- Add images, pop-up sounds, and/or music
- Add subtle background music when someone's talking
- Add interesting annotations that are not links
- Add annotation links only at the end of the video
- Make every ending different (a surprise, unique fact, something funny) to train your viewer to watch to the end

Video Duration Impact on Ranking

Most people want to know if the length of a video impacts rankings and should they make short (defined by YouTube as under four minutes) or long (defined by YouTube as twenty minutes or more) videos.

YouTube is fast paced. People want information quickly or they move on. If all factors were equal, it's fairly safe to assume that a user would choose a shorter video over a longer one.

Here's what we do know. We know retention rate plays a role in rankings. In most cases, it's more difficult to hold a visitor's attention during a longer video. Because of this, we can lean toward the idea that longer videos would have a lower retention rate, and thus, longer videos would rank lower in search results.

It's not just that visitors might get bored and click away. Recall that viewers can use *Filters* to actually search for short or long videos. If your video is 4.01 minutes long, you just missed the cut-off for filtered short video results. If you're filtered out, you lost your opportunity for a conversion.

You're going to have to do some research. Make predictions based on other videos in your niche and also do some testing to see what converts better for you. The video with the most views may not convert the best. It depends on the audience watching.

Does your buying audience prefer short or long? It does you no good to rank number one for long videos, if your target audience prefers short.

Another strategy is to make fast paced videos. Not so fast that the user leaves, but just fast enough so the user might want to rewind and replay, or even better, watch the entire video over again (and you gain another view).

On fast paced videos, you might remind the visitor in the audio that they can hit the pause button to freeze the screen at any moment. Tell them, "Hit pause to take notes."

Now that we've leaned toward short videos, let's not forget that a user seeking information will usually sit through *any length* of video as long as it continues to provide value all the way through. You can browse YouTube's longer videos that have significant numbers of views and try to determine how they maintain a viewer's attention.

How long should my video be? The answer is: as long as it takes to convey your valuable message, and not a second longer.

Authority: Social, Quality, and Klout Score

Your authority is a rating or value that supposedly deals with how much influence you have over others. This concept is also referred to as Social, Quality, or Klout Score. In general, these terms all track the same thing. They measure how active you are in social media, how active your followers are, how they interact with you, and how everyone's ratings connect together for a certain niche.

Your time can be better spent elsewhere than pursuing a better score. However, you should still know some best practices that will supposedly influence your score in a positive manner. Things that may impact your score are:

- Consistency and frequency of posting
- Your own activity (comments, shares, etc.) on YouTube
- Audience retention (*Watch Time*)
- Number of subscribers
- Number of views and Likes
- Video responses
- Viewer comments (even a poor comment is better than no comments)
- Number of shares and/or embeds of your video
- The niche of the site that embedded your video
- The niche of the people you connect to
- The rating score of the people you connect to

Your marketing efforts can play a role in addressing many of these factors. When you review your target audience, you might try to predict the actions they will take (such as sharing and commenting), and focus your efforts there. Social interactions are mini-conversions that take place along the way to a larger or final sales conversion.

We will review how to increase these social factors next. However, it's worth a reminder here, that your ultimate goal is not your social rating but profit conversions, so be careful not to get sidetracked.

Increase Views

Your total channel views, as well as the number of views on individual videos, will play a role in how well you rank. More views contributes to relevancy and to a higher position in search results. This means more exposure for your business.

Sharing

The fastest way to increase your views is through sharing. Sharing goes beyond social media. Keep in mind sharing can take place any time someone says, "Look at this" which can happen surrounding a TV, at a home computer, in a classroom, or in an office setting.

You want to anticipate why your audience will share a video. Is it funny, creative, unique, sentimental, or emotional? Is there anything unexpected? What type of video does your audience share and can you make more like that?

Checklist of Ideas to Increase Your Views

Preparation

1. Have a great thumbnail image to entice users to click.

2. Add 1x1 inch banner to your blog sidebar with "Watch our videos," or "Free training videos."

3. End your video with a statement like: "This was a follow-up to our video on … which you can view by clicking here." Add an annotation link.

4. Create fast short videos which will encourages viewers to hit pause, rewind, and/or watch again.

5. Schedule videos to go live during busy times. Begin with Wednesdays or Thursdays between 12-1 p.m or 3 p.m. Pacific Time. Then try Sunday mornings. Test for results.

6. Schedule your video to run every quarter on Facebook.

On YouTube

7. Group your videos as playlists which will rank on YouTube and become indexed in search engines.

8. Link one video to another with annotations and/or in the description.

9. Find a related video on YouTube that permits you to post a video response.

10. If you have more than one YouTube channel, cross promote using *Featured Channels*.

11. Find a channel with a similar audience and promote each other's channel in the *Featured Channels* section.

12. Refresh a stale video by altering the keywords , changing the category, and/or description.

On Yours and Others' Websites

13. Embed each video on several pages of your website.

14. Embed your video slightly above the fold to catch the visitor's eye.

15. Instant play: Embed videos on your website and code them for instant play, where they will begin playing as soon as the visitor arrives on the page. (Use this with caution, as some visitors may not be receptive to this.)

16. Create review videos and add them to the navigation or sidebars of pages with that or a related product.

17. Promote with Press Releases.
    Try http://www.kprweb.com.

18. Write guest blog posts and include your embedded video along with a link to your website and/or YouTube channel. (Be careful not to overdo this because your primary concern is creating content for your own site.)

List Building and Social Strategies

19. Increase marketing efforts to bring in more subscribers.

20. Autoresponder: Use your email platform autoresponder to send a video at one point in the funnel path or set it up so subscribers filter through all your videos over a certain time period.

21. Add your video to your newsletter or email list with an announcement that your video is now live and *an image* linking to your video on your blog (first choice) or on YouTube (second choice).

22. End your emails with something like, "In case you missed it, click here to see our video on… "

23. Add a video to every thank-you page whether it's for subscribing or for a purchase.

24. Share to social media networks, including LinkedIn.

25. Ask viewers to share your video.

26. Offer something extra for sharing your video.

27. Mention someone and share to them: Tell someone they are mentioned in a video, and in many cases that person will want to share the video to their own connections

28. Use natural paid advertising such as:

    - AdWords for Video
    - Facebook Fan Page Promoted Posts

RSS Feed

An RSS feed is a bit of coding that pulls a stream of information. You may have seen feeds in use online, when you saw a listing of current Twitter posts displayed on a website.

In the case of YouTube, an RSS feed can pull all your video uploads. This can be powerful when put to use for promoting, marketing, seeking views, and increasing subscribers.

To see your RSS feed for all your YouTube activity (uploads, playlist additions, comments, likes, shares, and so forth), use the following URL (but change *yourusername* to your channel's name): http://www.YouTube.com/user/*yourusername*/feed

If This then That (IFTTT)

As you learn more about feeds, you will come across many unique uses of feeds to connect with customers. One website that uses feeds is: *If This then That* at http://ifttt.com/.

This website allows you to make *Recipes* of automated actions. For example, in setting up your channel, we explained that YouTube automatic posting goes to a Facebook Profile and not a Facebook Page (business page). This can be solved using an IFTTT scheduling Recipe that says "If I upload to YouTube, then make a posting to my Facebook Page." Once set, this saves you time posting to your Facebook Page. The recipe appears as a diagram and you can edit it at anytime.

Google Gadget

You can embed your RSS feed into any site using the coding for a Google Gadget mini video player (shown below). Your visitor can click the arrows to choose a video to watch. See a live example at: http://www.kidsandmoneytoday.com/about/

To put the RSS video feed player on your html website or insert it on your blog, use the coding below. You will need to change *YourChannelName* to your YouTube username.

To use this in a WordPress sidebar, add a text widget to your sidebar and copy the coding into the widget.

```
<script src="http://www.gmodules.com/ig/
ifr?URL=http://www.Google.com/ig/modules/YouTube.
xml&amp;up_channel=YourChannelName&amp;synd=open&a
mp;w=320&amp;h=390&amp;title=&amp;border=%23ffffff%7
C3px%2C1px+solid+%23999999&amp;output=js"></script>
```
[4]

To copy and paste this coding, visit our resource page at http://www.KidsandMoneyToday.com/video-resources/

---

4. Zishan, Mohasin, Shaanhaider.com, GeekyStuffs, *HOW TO : Embed YouTube Video Channel Feed In Your Blog*, http://www.shaanhaider.com/2011/04/embed-youtube-video-channel-feed-in.html

Encourage Comments

Comments are one way YouTube measures the importance of your video. You can increase your comments by:

1. *Connecting Emotionally:* When your video makes an emotional connection with the viewer, they are more likely to leave a comment.

2. *Responding:* Try to respond to every comment. Everyone likes to be acknowledged and your commenters may eventually share, subscribe, or return to make more comments. In general, don't delete negative comments unless they contain profanity. Instead, respond by saying, "Thank you for sharing your point of view" or "Thank you for pointing that out," and leave it at that.

3. *Mentioning Someone*: In many cases this person will come back and post a thank you in your comment area.

4. *Consistency*: When you become part of someone's routine schedule, they become comfortable with you and will be more likely to comment.

Disable Comments

If you choose to disable comments on your channel, you will sacrifice some ranking juice. Comments are an indicator of channel activity and without them, viewers obviously interact less, so your video may rank lower in search results.

You might disable comments simply because you don't have the time to moderate them. Another reason might be that you anticipate offensive comments due to your niche subject area, and you don't want to turn other viewers away.

You might also want to push all comments to your blog. If so, explain this immediately in your description with a direct link to your blog post. One reason to encourage comments on your blog is to maintain full control and contact with the viewer. If you ever close your YouTube account, at least you would have all comments associated with that channel or video retained on your blog.

Expand Your Subscriber List

To quickly see your list of subscribers, log into your YouTube channel, and type http://www.YouTube.com/subscribers in your browser. (There are other ways to arrive here but this is fast and usually reliable.)

Recall that YouTube users can choose to keep subscriptions private. If I have my privacy set to "Keep all my subscriptions private," then when I subscribe to your channel, you will not see me on your subscriber list.

The only notification you have of subscribers who have chosen to hide their subscriptions is the email you receive. This contains their username (but not their email). If you are interested in these people, save your *New Subscriber* email notifications. Learn more about them using this URL (change *username* to your subscribers name): http://www.YouTube.com/user/*username*/feed.

Viewers can subscribe to you even if they do not have a channel. When this person subscribes, you'll receive a message like:

> "A new user has subscribed to you on YouTube! They don't have a YouTube channel yet, but they will still receive notifications when you upload new videos, create playlists, like videos, and so on."

Encourage Subscribers

The main message you need to convey is to *convince* viewers *why* they need to subscribe. Do this and subscribers will come naturally and you will have a very *targeted* list.

A common practice to build a list of subscribers is to offer something for free for clicking the subscribe button. This can be highly effective, but it also builds a less targeted list. Some people will use fake emails, and some people will unsubscribe immediately after receiving your free offer.

Never pay for someone to subscribe, and never pay others to solicit subscribers for you. You want true targeted subscribers.

As you build your list, remember that the true measure of success is your Return on Investment. Your focus is conversions. A large subscriber list means little if you can't convert it to sales.

That being said, a large untargeted list will still help with your authority (social) ratings and appearance, and this helps boost your channel's credibility. You have to find the sweet spot to have an effective list that will bring you successful conversions.

Checklist of Ideas to Increase Subscribers

1. Use a good description on your channel. Explain what it's about and why people should subscribe.

2. Create an awesome Channel Trailer (the first video your unsubscribed visitors will see).

3. Ask viewers to subscribe in the audio of your video. Tell them why they should subscribe and how to do it.

4. Ask in your video annotations and *Description* area.

5. Add a subscribe link or widget to your blog in several locations (and code it so you can tell which location performs best).

6. Send your subscribers to a thank-you page after subscribing and on that page, invite them to share with their friends. (Maybe offer a bonus for sharing.)

7. Be consistent in posting and people will subscribe so as not to miss your weekly or monthly video.

8. Offer to take an action for reaching a subscriber goal such as, "I will do xxx when I reach # of subscribers." (make a donation, shave your head, hold a free webinar, post childhood pictures, or other creative idea)

9. Subscribe to other channels and often they immediately subscribe back.

10. Increase your social interaction within YouTube.

11. Tease visitors within your video. Ask them to "subscribe now" so they don't miss the upcoming video on...

12. Give partial information in your video and direct the viewer to find the rest on your blog. Post what you promised on the blog and while they are there, ask them to join your blog's email list. (Subscribe to the blog.)

13. Use LeadPlayer to display your and other people's videos to increase blog subscribers. Find LeadPlayer at http://www.kidsandmoneytoday.com/video-player (affiliate link)

14. Link to the YouTube Opt-in *confirmation* subscription URL in your video description, website, blog, social media, or newsletter. Change *UserName* to your YouTube channel in this URL:

http://YouTube.com/subscription_center?add_user=*UserName*

15. Tease by posting a thumbnail image of an upcoming video to any social media site, along with a text description and a direct link to subscribe in order to be notified when the video goes live.

16. Facebook Images: Upload your thumbnail image with a link to your YouTube subscribe URL, which encourages them to subscribe prior to watching.

17. Give something for FREE when they click subscribe. You might try these ideas:
    - PDF file of tips for something
    - Royalty Free images if you're an artist
    - Royalty Free music if you're a musician
    - Training (might be video format, CDs, or DVDs)
    - Consultation from you
    - Annual or lifetime membership to your program
    - Blog post for their website
    - Discount coupon for a product of yours or someone else's (joint promotion)

18. Announce a live streaming Hangout (also called a Video Call; discussed later) and ask visitors to subscribe to participate or watch in the future.

Your Pay Raise is in Your Analytics

Too often, companies begin with video creation and then ask, "How can I rank my video?" As we've explained thus far, the best path to ranking for a targeted audience is to establish goals, identify customers and what they search for, and create video content that matches their keyword search terms.

All of your efforts will be to no avail if you don't check your analytics. Your reports tell you what is working and what isn't. Your reports let you know if you are bringing traffic to your website and what method is growing your lists.

All the ideas thus far should be creating step-by-step conversions for you along your sales path. If you check your analytics and make changes, the impact should be like receiving a bump in pay raise.

You want to measure each step of your conversion path. Are views and click throughs increasing? How long did the user spend on the landing page? This type of information will tell you what's succeeding and where the user left your conversion path.

In channel setup, you connected your channel with analytics. We did this early on so your data would already be accumulating and available when you're ready to begin evaluation. We don't want to view our reports for vanity sake. By that we mean, these reports are not *look and feel good (or bad) reports*. Instead we want to use them to take action.

Recall our marketing discussion about making a prediction from an analysis of variables. Taking action means evaluating your current state of affairs and making a decision with a *predicted outcome* as a result of this decision. You should answer two questions:

1. Change: What will you do that you predict will increase your performance?

2. Evaluation: When you made a change, did it work?

Rank Tracker - WordPress Plugin

If you use WordPress, there is a fairly cheap plugin ($17.01 as of Spring 2013) that allows you to track rankings in both YouTube and Google. You can find this plugin at our affiliate link. Go to: http://www.kidsandmoneytoday.com/video-rank.

Some advantages of this plugin are:

1. View your rankings for both Google and YouTube right inside your blog, together in one location

2. Set how often your report will be updated. Once a day or twice a day is recommended.

3. Track up to 25 keywords per blog using the free version. (If you follow our recommendation for one keyword per video, this means you can track 25 videos per blog.)

4. Track unlimited keywords after paying an upgrade fee.

5. Simple and easy sort features: Sort by Keyword, YouTube Rank, Google Rank, or Position Change:

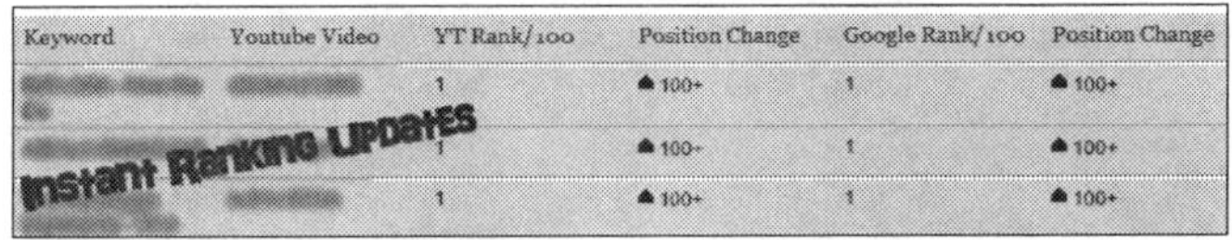

Keyword	Youtube Video	YT Rank/100	Position Change	Google Rank/100	Position Change
[illegible]	[illegible]	1	▲ 100+	1	▲ 100+
[illegible]	[illegible]	1	▲ 100+	1	▲ 100+
[illegible]	[illegible]	1	▲ 100+	1	▲ 100+

The YouTube Video column shows the ID for your video. This should not really be an issue because you should be able to identify the video simply by viewing the corresponding keyword column. If needed, you can click the ID (it's a link) and your video will appear in a pop-up window.

This is *live tracking*. There is no tracking over a time frame and no export feature. If you wish to monitor a video that waffles up and down in rankings, you will have to print the screen out as a hardcopy on different dates and compare your printed data.

Rank Tracker - Software

Rank Tracker is a software with a free rank checking version that you download and run on your computer. Visit our affiliate URL at: http://www.kidsandmoneytoday.com/rank-checker/.

(There are several companies online using the term "Rank Tracker" and many are paid options, so to see the one we recommend, follow our link.)

The free version has a limitation: the data cannot be saved. The paid upgrade for this capability is $99.75 (as of Spring 2013).

The software is very easy to use. You enter your YouTube video URL and choose the venue you wish to see rankings for. You would choose Google and YouTube, but they also have options for Yahoo, Bing, and several others as shown in the image:

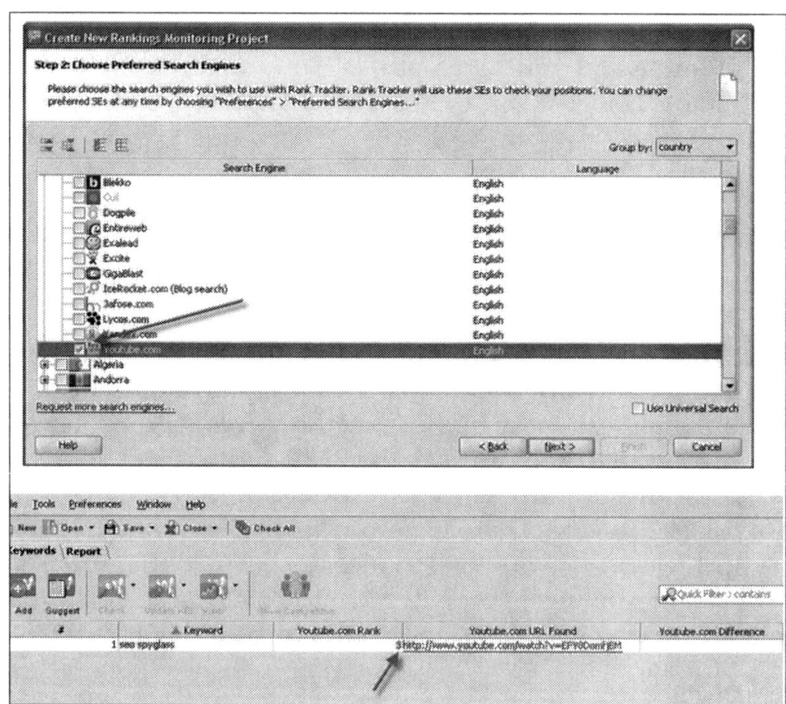

The software automatically pulls in your YouTube tags which you can edit, delete, or even add more. With one click and a small wait time, you have a list of how your video ranks for numerous keywords across multiple venues.

How are Rank Tracker and the Plugin Different?

The main differences from the WordPress plugin are:

1. Rank Tracker is a download that runs on your computer, so anyone can use it. The plugin is only available for WordPress users.

2. Rank Tracker presents a free version, although saving of files is not permitted. (Upgrade to the paid version if you wish to save data.)

3. Rank Tracker offers additional search engines to monitor.

4. Rank Tracker allows you to view one video with several keywords (as opposed to viewing all your videos at one time). While we recommend aiming at one keyword per video, this feature can be very helpful in tracking long-tail keywords. You might also identify videos that rank better for a keyword that you have actually targeted with a different video. In such a case, you might swap the focus of the videos.

5. In the software, you can only view one video at a time, so if you use WordPress and want a quick view of all videos in one place, you might want to use both options.

Trends

When you have had your videos up for a period of time, especially after a year, you can begin to look for trends. Are there peaks and valleys that can be narrowed down to specific days of the week, months, holidays, or promotions you ran? Evaluate what caused the peaks and valleys, make changes with predictions, and reevaluate. Watch for trends in daily life. What's popular on TV and YouTube, or at the mall, library, or fairs? Try to capitalize on this.

YouTube Analytics

One of the first things you might notice in your analytics is the *Overview* shows data for your entire channel. You can view this data for any set time frame of your choice (custom, last 30 days, all the way up to lifetime data.)

Where do you see the views for a specific video?

See your report:

- Go to *YouTube Analytics > Views Report > Views*
- Choose your date range
- Use the search box to choose your video

To see the views of an individual video, choose Views from the left menu and click inside the search box (see the next image) to reveal a dropdown menu of your videos. Choose a video.

Sample (Partial) Report

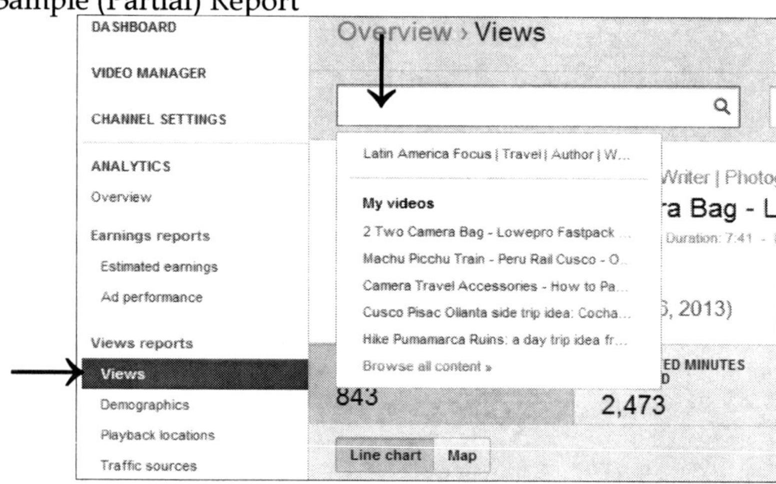

Take Action: Decide what you might do to increase your views. Record the date you make the change and come back to see if your prediction was correct. Adjust as needed. (One simple method to track your changes is to print the screen, mark the printout with the change you are making and today's date. Place this in a binder to monitor over a period of time.)

How is your video found?

See your report:

- Go to *YouTube Analytics* > *Views Report* > *Traffic Sources*
- Use the search box to choose your video

The *Traffic Sources* report helps you identify how people are finding your video. For example, you might see YouTube search, Google search, and External Website.

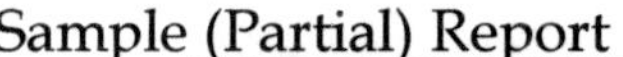

Sample (Partial) Report

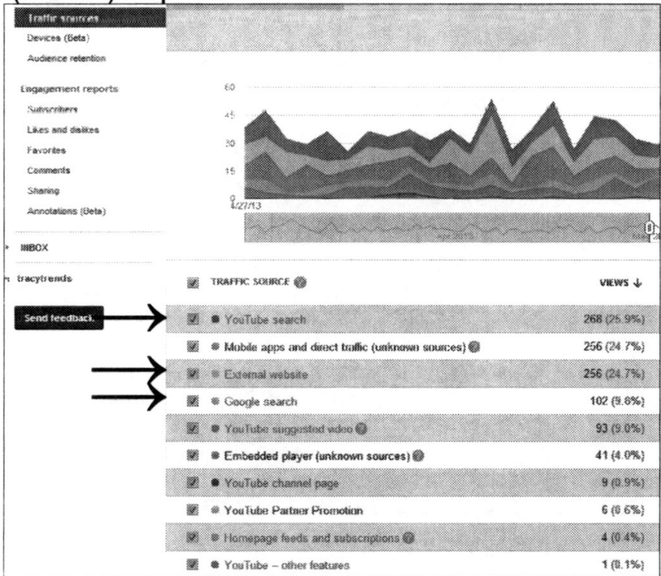

Take Action: Decide what area you might like to increase. For example: suppose you want to increase views from *YouTube suggested video,* which are the related videos that appear on the side of other videos. You might takes steps to connect your video to others on YouTube. You could check their description for words you might add to your *Tags* or *Description*. Any idea that would connect your video to others, should help increase these types of views. Brainstorm for other ideas for improvement. (Note the action and date of your changes so you can monitor what works.)

What external websites send you traffic?

See your report:

- Go to *YouTube Analytics* > *Views Report* >*Traffic Sources* > *External Website*
- Use the search box to choose your video

This is where you see any site that sent you traffic. It might include your own website, Google, Bing, and social media sites like: Facebook, Twitter, Zazzle, and Meetup.

Sample (Partial) Report (views and minutes watched not shown)

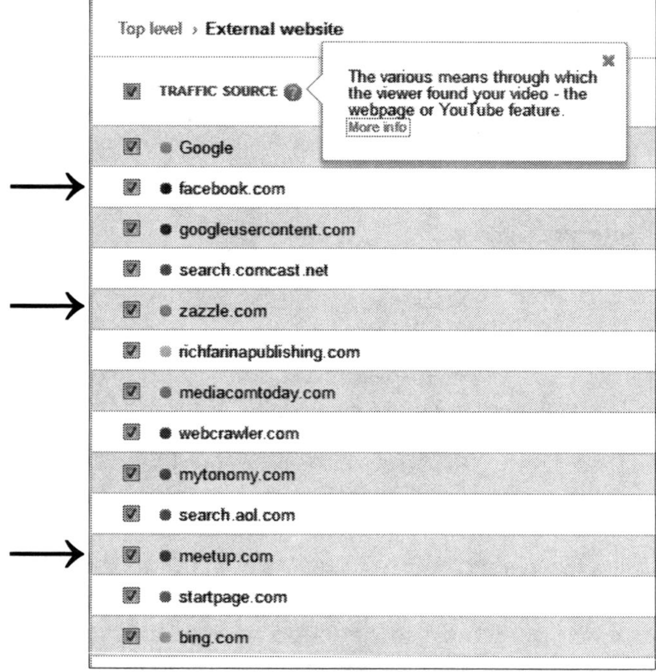

Take Action: Evaluate what you would like to increase. Perhaps increase activity on a social site that brings in traffic that's converting. You might also write more guest posts on a blog sending traffic. (As with the other reports, note the date of your changes to monitor progress.)

Where are your videos embedded?

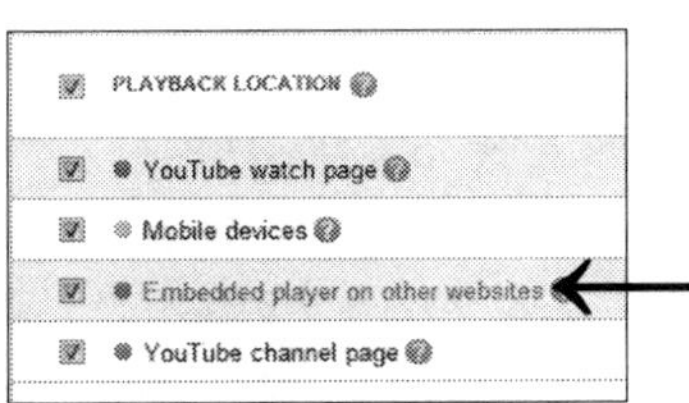

See your report:

- Go to *YouTube Analytics* > *Views Report* > *Playback Locations* > *Embedded Player on Other Websites*
- Use the search box to choose your video

Take Action: What type of sites provide the most views? Try to connect with them or invite similar sites to embed your videos.

What keywords were used on YouTube to find you?

See your report:

- Go to *YouTube Analytics* > *Traffic Sources* > *YouTube Search*
- Use the search box to choose your video

View the keywords visitors used to find your video.

Sample (Partial) Report

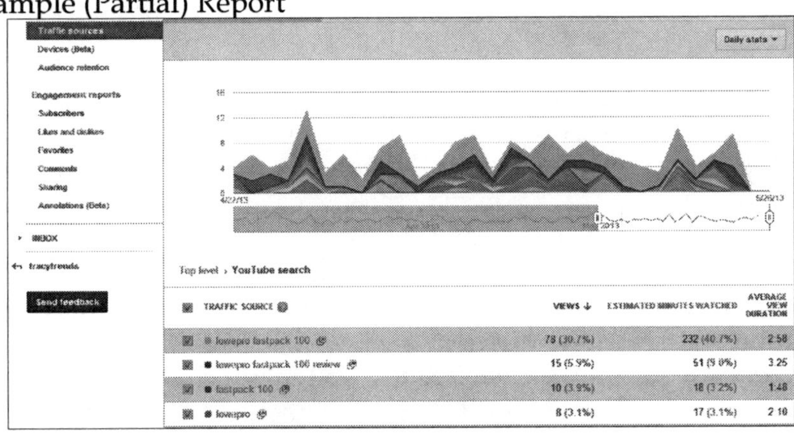

Take Action: Are users finding you with the keywords you targeted? Are there new keywords listed that you might add to your *Descriptions* or *Tags*? Could you make a new video or write an article for the new keywords? Is a video being found for keywords that you expected another video to rank for?

How are viewers interacting with your annotations?

See your report:

- Go to *YouTube Analytics* > *Engagement Reports* > *Annotations*
- Use the search box to choose your video

Check which annotations are being clicked.

Sample (Partial) Report

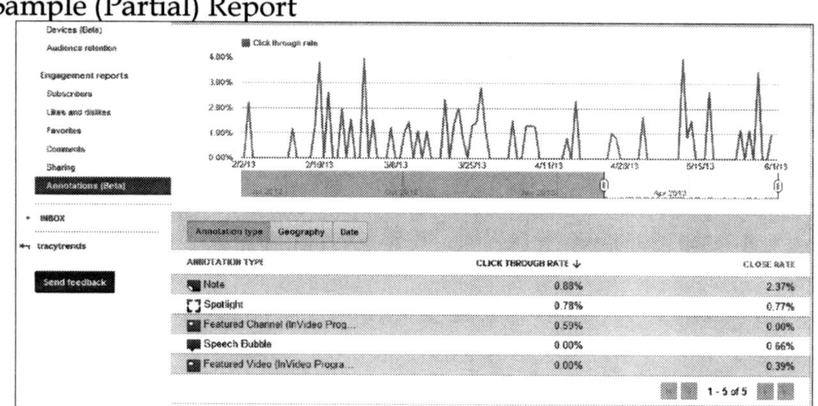

Take Action:

This report includes your Featured Channel and Featured Video overlays, which you may recall—can be distracting. If they are not being clicked, you might turn them off.

Check your *Close Rate* for your annotations, meaning the viewer turned them off. You might remove, relocate, or change the length of time on these annotations.

Look at your *Click Through Rates*. You might change the type of annotation to see if one pulls better interaction than another. Are Spotlights performing better than Notes? Should you relocate an annotation?

Note the date of your changes to monitor progress.

What videos were shared and how many times?

See your report:

- Go to *YouTube Analytics* > *Engagement Reports* > *Sharing*
- Use the search box to choose your video

We mentioned how important interaction is in ranking videos. This report helps monitor your success with this algorithm factor.

Sample (Partial) Report

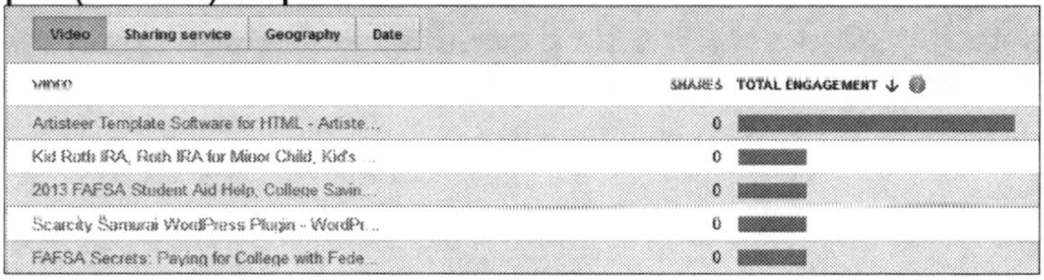

Video | Sharing service | Geography | Date

VIDEO	SHARES	TOTAL ENGAGEMENT ↓
Artisteer Template Software for HTML - Artiste...	0	
Kid Roth IRA, Roth IRA for Minor Child, Kid's ...	0	
2013 FAFSA Student Aid Help, College Savin...	0	
Scarcity Samurai WordPress Plugin - WordPr...	0	
FAFSA Secrets: Paying for College with Fede...	0	

Take Action:

You can see the number of times a video was shared and if you click on the video, you will see the sharing service that was used. Repeat strategies that work.

Even if your shares are zero (as shown here), you should have activity in your Total Engagement column. This includes other YouTube social activity for the video: a sum of all likes, dislikes, favorites added and removed, shares, comments, and subscribes and unsubscribes.

Where are people subscribing?

See your report:

- Go to *Analytics* > *Engagement Reports* > *Subscribers*
- Use the search box to choose your video

Take Action: In this report you can see which video generates new subscribers. Compare your different video types, such as emotional, self-help, inspirational, educational, etc. and make more of the type that converts best.

How well do you maintain your audience's attention?

See your report:

- Go to *YouTube Analytics* > *Views Reports* >*Audience Retention*
- Use the search box to choose your video

Check your viewer *Watch Time*. Recent YouTube tutorials indicate that YouTube's algorithm is placing more and more emphasis on this factor. (Note: Your Average Percentage Viewed can actually go over 100% as a result of your viewer rewinding portions of your video.) The initial report will list each video with two columns as shown in the image.

Sample (Partial) Report (video and minutes watched not shown)

AVERAGE VIEW DURATION	AVERAGE PERCENTAGE VIEWED
1:09	48.0%
1:53	58.3%
1:16	45.3%
0:31	64.0%
0:26	57.5%
0:34	83.9%
0:13	91.8%

Take Action: If audience retention is particularly low on a video, consider deleting it and uploading a new one. The negative impact of a bad video outweighs any benefit you might be receiving from its age, views, and embedded videos. It's a weed growing in your business, attracting unwanted attention, and reducing your authority and relevance. Cut it and move forward.

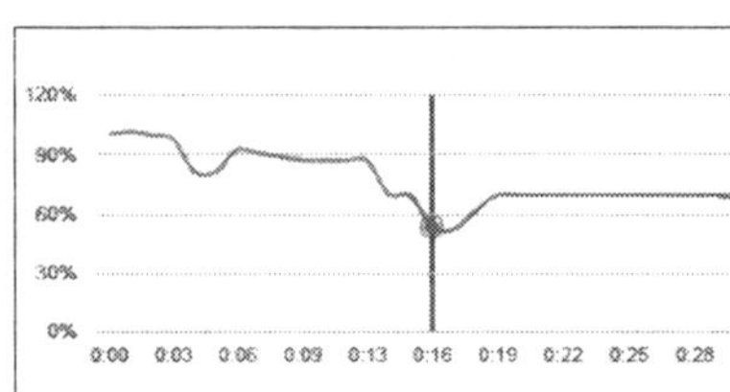

Click on an individual video and look for any drop offs. This is where your users are leaving. Do you have an annotation link to your website there? Then this drop off should be a good thing.

If not, you might add a new annotation just prior to a drop-off time-frame to entice the viewer to watch longer. Also look for high points of engagement, and add *Calls to Action* there. (Record the date of any changes you make.)

Google Analytics

What social networks are sending visitors to my website?

Your Google Analytics coding will track all visits from social media networks, which includes YouTube. Watch your statistics from Pinterest, Twitter, Google+, and Facebook too, especially if you are posting videos there with direct links to your website (as opposed to posting with a link to your YouTube channel). The Overview Report quickly tells you the networks sending traffic. If you have Goals set up, the report will also show the number of conversions from this social traffic.

See your report:

- Go to *Google Analytics > Traffic Sources > Social > Overview*

Sample Report

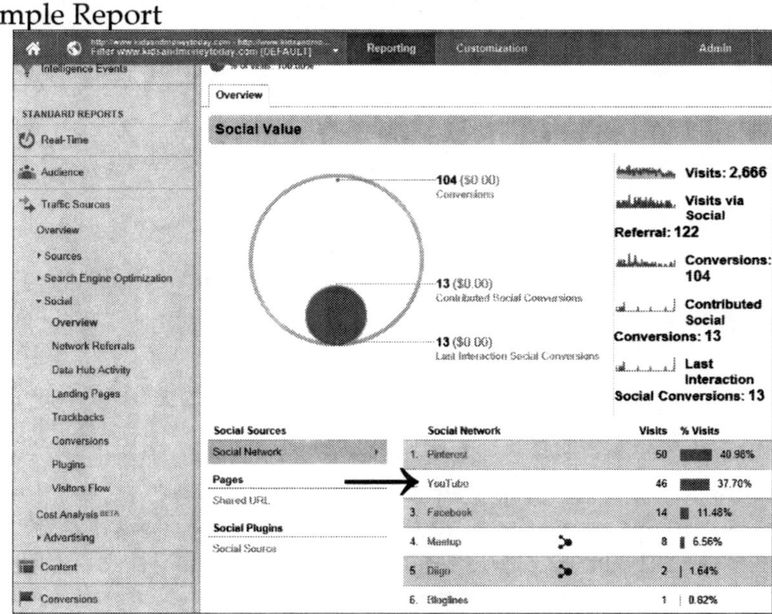

Take Action: Click on a specific social network and you will see the URLs that were shared on that site. Try to figure out why certain videos sent more traffic, and create more videos like that.

What social networks are converting for me?

See your report:

- Go to *Google Analytics* > *Traffic Sources* > *Social* > *Conversions*

If you show no social data, widen the date range or check you analytics coding. Google has a Social Data Hub of participants including: Digg, Disqus, Reddit, and more. See the full list at: http://developers.Google.com/analytics/devguides/socialdata/

To track the monetary value of your social conversions, you set up Goals inside your Google Analytics account. Goals are set up at the *Profile* level found at *Admin* > *Property ID* > *Profile* > *Goals*. A goal can be something as simple as landing on a page or more complex, like completing a form or downloading a PDF. You can also set a monetary value for each goal. If you don't, the report shows zero for the conversion value (as in the report below).

Sample Report (of 6 YouTube conversions with zero value)

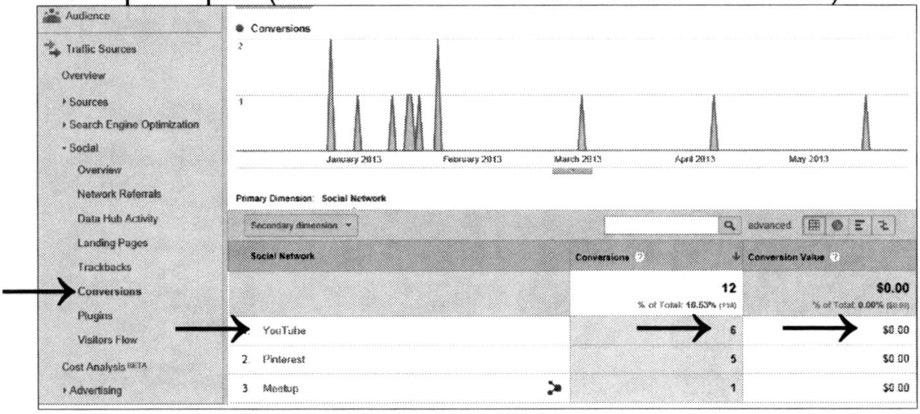

Take Action: A monetary value will add to your evaluation of social networks. It might help you decide if more time should be devoted to YouTube or to other networks. For larger companies, this could tell you which social network requires the focus of three employees, instead of one.

You can add second dimensions (such as landing pages) to your Conversion Reports to provide even more evaluation. Conversion Reports can also help track your social media promotions.

(Record the date of any changes you make, and come back to see if your prediction was correct. Adjust as needed.)

Which social media site sends engaging visitors?

See your report:

- Go to *Google Analytics > Traffic Sources > Social > Network Referrals*

View your *Network Referrals* report to see engagement metrics like: Visits, PageViews, Average Visit Duration, and Pages/Visit.

Sample Report

Social Network	Visits ↓	Pageviews	Avg Visit Duration	Pages / Visit
1. Pinterest	50	97	00:01:12	1.94
2. YouTube ⟵	46	111	00:01:10	2.41
3. Facebook	14	29	00:00:52	2.07
4. Meetup	8	20	00:03:04	2.50
5. Diigo	2	4	00:00:02	2.00
6. Bloglines	1	2	00:00:02	2.00
7. Twitter	1	10	00:05:27	10.00

Take Action: This report might help identify the type of audience you're attracting. Compare it with your conversions. Is a social site sending you 1,000 visitors who spend a lot of time reading (indicated by duration on the site or visiting many pages), but only a small percentage convert? What might cause this?

Is anyone clicking your YouTube Description links?

If you don't like reading reports or initially, just want something simple and easy to monitor your data, then you might choose to use a URL shortener or Redirect Coding. This shortens a very long URL into a nice short URL and records clicks. When you use a URL shortener, you can bypass Google analytics and just review your data using the software itself.

Two popular and free URL link shorteners are Google's shortener at http://goo.gl/ and Bitly found at http://www.bitly.com.

If you are using WordPress, you can usa a Plugin. Our affiliate link: http://www.kidsandmoneytoday.com/track-link will take you to the plugin we use. (There is a one time fee.)

Your Repeatable Video System

Here's a quick summary of concepts we've covered. For a successful Video Marketing Plan, you should know:

- What you want your visitor to do,
- What keywords they use to look for solutions,
- What your targeted customer wants emotionally,
- What your plan is to rank well,
- Where you will post your video for exposure,
- How you will measure the success of each video

A Video Marketing Plan is different from a Repeatable Video System. The plan is about marketing. The system is about your production process. You want to have an efficient, repeatable production process. As your income grows, you can entertain the idea of outsourcing certain aspects of this process.

A good strategy for creating videos is to produce groups of videos together. This has been referred to as the shotgun approach, batch processing, or segment processing.

In a factory, you see ten people completing a task in an assembly line, but each person is actually doing the same task again and again. You have to decide what is better: segment processing or one-by-one completion? The presumption is that segment processing (completing several instances of a task) is most efficient.

The main tasks for video are: idea, script, film, edit, upload, and promote. You might set a time frame to write video ideas, the focus, the *Call to Action,* and how you will measure the video's success.

In the next segment, write the script for each video idea.

In the next time frame, you will film all the videos. (Change your clothes between takes or wear branded clothing, so when you upload your videos, it will look as though each one was filmed on a different day.)

Prioritize the filming by beginning with the least important video. As you film, the audio, techniques, and how natural your voice sounds will all improve, so when segment processing (or batch processing), save your most important video to film last.

In the editing segment, you might link videos together or reuse clips across videos.

The final segment of your video system would be uploading, scheduling, optimization, and sharing.

The benefit of segment processing is that you can eventually outsource a segment. Outsourcing may be difficult if you love to create the video, love to try different audio, to experiment with lighting, and so on. But to really grow a business, we usually need to transition out of the creation process and learn to delegate.

Batch processing videos works well, but it should only be done *after* you have completed your first few videos and only done in *small batches*. The benefits of completing one job at a time is actually *more efficient* for *business growth*. This is because you:

- Don't waste time changing your train of thought from the message of one video to the next.
- Find and learn from mistakes early. (You don't want to be editing 20 videos and then, discover a recording issue.)
- Gain the psychological satisfaction and motivation from finishing a job through to completion.
- Go live on YouTube sooner.

Plan Your Video

Completion, Quality, and Quantity

Videos are like writing or designing websites, the piece can almost always be improved. At some point, you will have to decide what is "good enough" or "a good start" for the action you wish to accomplish and make the decision to upload and go live. Your business objective is targeted traffic, not the perfect video.

With every video or book or seminar (if you attend them), you will learn something new, and it's important to allow yourself to learn as you grow. Completion *always* trumps quality and quantity. Completion brings conversions.

This doesn't mean you should upload low quality boring videos of no value. Quality will impact your ranking, and you want to be found. Instead, this means to accept the fact that your videos will not be perfect and will always have room to improve. Don't wait around for perfection.

How Much Free Information?

The biggest concern we hear again and again is, "I don't want to give away too much for free." This is often heard from those selling a course or a reference book. The same answer we hear recommended again and again is, "Do not to worry about giving away too much for free in your videos."

Focus on your target audience. Some people will only come for the free information. Accept this and realize that these people never were and will never be your target audience. Your ideal customer is not the one with the mindset of, "I can do this myself without purchasing."

If you sold apples, and a visitor arrived looking for pears and walked away, you would not feel badly. It may help to view your "freebie" viewers in this manner. Don't worry that they came, watched, and left. At most, they are considered your top funnel customers, if you can even declare them in your funnel at all. They were never interested in what you are selling. Let them go.

And if you're fortunate, this freebie audience will still mention your business or share your video. After all, who wouldn't tell their friends about this great free information your video just provided? This can result in some untraceable word-of-mouth marketing for you.

As a precaution, you should always try to include your branding on products and videos. Put a logo in every video, and if your video offers a free PDF, include your business information at the top and bottom of every PDF page. If the PDF is passed to 100 friends, then at least you gain some business exposure.

Giving valuable free information ultimately builds your trust and credibility. When you present this free information, try to include a reason to also own the product, become a member, or purchase the service. Let the viewer think, "I needed it for reference" or "I knew I would receive additional quality information with a membership."

Your video should make the viewers feel that the information was so valuable, they can't wait to have more. If you can send them the message that they will miss out by not signing up or purchasing, you should have even higher conversions.

Train yourself toward a new way of thinking. Ask, "What can I give away for free today, that will bring in future sales?"

Prioritize

Every business decision should be made thinking about:

1. Profitability,

2. Ease of implementation, and

3. Repetitiveness

As mentioned in the Goals and Conversions chapter, emotion is not on this list. You might use a spreadsheet to create a video-to-do list as a means to rank and prioritize your videos. This will help keep your decision making analytical rather than emotional.

Our sample spreadsheet lists the video ideas with corresponding columns for: profit rating, ease of use, and repetitiveness. (Use your own opinion to add ratings from 1 to 10.) Sum these values across and work on the video with the highest value first.

Sample spreadsheet:

Video Idea	Profit	Ease	Repeatable	Value (sum)
A	5	2	10	17
B	9	9	1	19
C	2	9	9	20

Your *Profit* value might show 5 for a 50 percent profit, 9 would be 90 percent, and so on.

The *Ease* column represents how easy it is to make the video. If your video involves another person, it is more difficult. It is even more difficult should you have to film from the air, which might mean you will hire a pilot and cover the expense of an airplane.

Repeatable means either the video produces consistent monthly cash, or the system itself is repeatable (such as a template video where you can easily create more videos by simply changing a slide or clip). You could even separate these two thoughts into two unique columns, and you might even want to create additional column factors to incorporate your own value ideas.

In the spreadsheet above, video C, which actually ranks as the least profitable, would be worked on first, because it is easy to make and is in some manner, repeatable. Sometimes, consistent fast cash can be a higher priority than a one time profit at some date in the future.

Get Creative

You can add variety to your videos by changing the setting. Try indoors, outdoors, a flat background, long hallway, or green screen. Change your clothes and music, or include production bloopers. Try using black and white footage. Film into a mirror or out in the rain. Purchase a special effect clip. Use animation. You might browse photography magazines to obtain inspiration.

Video Duration for Viewer Retention

Recall that earlier, we discussed the length of your video in relation to ranking and our recommendation was to aim for short videos. The YouTube visitor seems to be even more impatient than our typical website visitor. Get to the point quickly.

A popular video structure to compel a viewer to complete a *Call to Action* is to use a sandwich approach. This means you will have some sort of introduction, a middle, and a closure.

You can create a double layer sandwich by using branding as an additional layer in the beginning (actually in position two) and near the end. Your video outline might look something like this:

- 6-10 second attention grabber
- 5-10 second brand introduction
- 5-10 second topic introduction (introduce the context, explain what's coming; convince the viewer to watch)
- 1-2 minute content
- 5-10 second *Call to Action* closure
- 6-10 second brand ending (outtake)

Remember the advanced YouTube search has a filter cut-off of four minutes for short videos, so watch your segments carefully during planning, production, and editing.

Your batch processing might include creating clips for your brand introduction and outtakes. These clips can be inserted into any video. If you make them templates, you can refresh them with minor adjustments. For example, if your logo drops in after 10 seconds, maybe six months from now, you would alter it to make your logo fade in, and six months later, change it again.

Also alter your endings. Occasionally place something after your branding message such as a blooper or other surprise. This trains your viewer to watch to the end.

Channel Trailer

Your channel trailer is a video shown only to unsubscribed visitors to your channel. It's usually used for branding and to increase subscribers. It should be one of the first videos you create and updated as needed.

Your channel trailer appears as the first video below your channel banner (as shown below). To the immediate right of your trailer is a block of text. This text comes from the *description of the video you set as your trailer.* This text should explain what you do and why someone might subscribe.

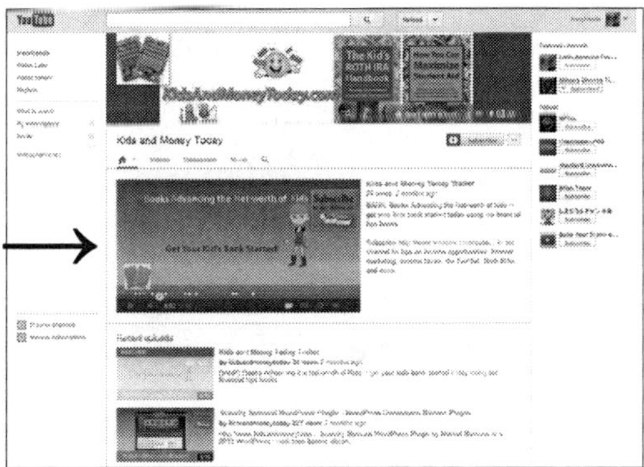

To set your channel trailer, click the Channel Trailer button beneath your banner and choose the video you want to appear. You can always change or remove your trailer.

Once a visitor subscribes, the network recognizes the user's status and the trailer video disappears. The middle of the screen then shows a suggested video and recent activity.

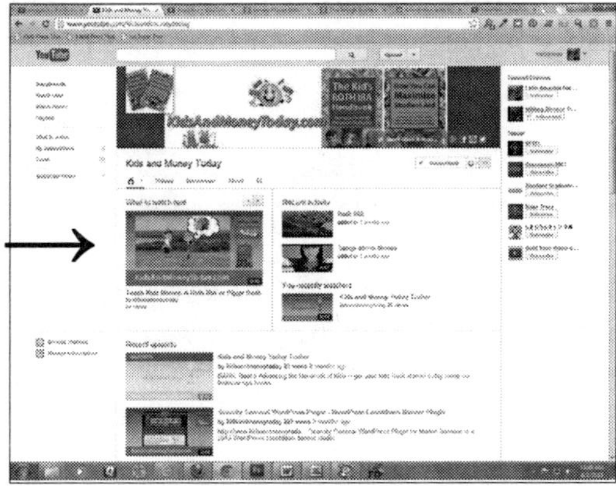

Checklist of Ideas for Video Topics, Types, or Themes

A good place to begin creating your video idea list is to use the questions you answered to identify your audience, along with your keyword research. Try these ideas for more inspiration:

Emotion

1. *Motivate:* Make a "You can do this…" video.

2. *Influence Others:* Create a video petition, call to write congress, elect a politician, etc..

3. *Collect Donations:* Do a video for a cause or charity.

Brand Building

4. *Branding*: Create a viedo establishing your expertise in this field (similar to education videos).

5. *About Page*: Tell how your business was started; include a direct connection to a product or service for sale.

6. *Promotions, Announcements, and Teasers:* Forecast upcoming products, future training videos, or a contest, event, new release, holiday sale, or special occasion.

Products or Service

7. *Sales Generation and/or Product Features:* Sell your product, service, or affiliate product.

8. *Educate:* Share knowledge, updates, news, documentary ideas, teaching, or training. (These usually target the audience in the research or learning phase of your sales funnel.)

9. *Information:* Give one tip and send the user to your website to learn more, or provide a direct link to purchase.

10. *Shopping Hauls:* Talk about your purchases (that relate to your product) as you unpack your shopping bag.

11. *Stories:* Tell a story of how someone used your product.

12. *How to*: Create problem solving videos where you offer solutions with resources and a link to a purchase page.

13. *Comparison Reviews:* Show one product or concept compared to another, and state the pros and cons.

14. *Testimonial or Endorsement Reviews:* Ask others to do a video review of your brand or product.

15. *Demonstration:* Similar to reviews or testimonials, but instead include a visual demonstration of unique, unusual, or funny ways to use your product or service.

16. *Quick Start Guide:* Make a video that's a visual representation of the printed quick start guide a customer might receive with a product purchase.

Customer Interaction

17. *Contest:* Announce your contest and collect viewer information when they participate.

18. *Quiz*: Make a video with questions and lead viewers to a landing page with answers.

19. *Increase Traffic:* Make videos where the primary purpose is a click through to your website.

20. *List Building or Lead Generation:* These videos increase your YouTube, blog, or newsletter subscriber list(s).

21. *Add Social Media Exposure:* Create videos with a strong message or reason for your audience to share them.

22. *Increase Customer Connection:* These types of videos are aimed at increasing views and comments. They might be controversial or indicate other reasons for users to talk.

23. *FAQ:* Have your video answer customer's Frequently Asked Questions.

24. *Decrease Customer Contact:* Create videos that teach, and as a result, decrease your customer support calls.

Sketch Your Story

Once you have a video idea, its goal and duration, make a short outline of what you are trying to accomplish. Think about your audience based on backgrounds and needs. Some viewers may already have knowledge on your subject, while others are beginners. When you attempt a video that will reach multiple levels, consider creating an introduction slide to quickly bring everyone up to speed. An opening slide might show the agenda or path to take. Longer videos might show this slide again midway through, to help viewers keep track of the progression of events.

Another approach to keep viewers with expertise interested, is to foreshadow or tease about the subject you will cover.

Your story sketch should be short. You will get into more detail in the next step, making the script. Sketch a "storyboard." Draw a box for each scene with a short description and *Call to Action.*

Think about how you tell a story. Stories keep the viewer engaged and help make videos successful. Stories are made up of problems or conflicts. They're engaging. Viewers can relate to the characters from their own personal experiences or experiences of their family, friends, and clients. Stories conclude with a solution or change (your *Call to Action*).

Your introduction sets the scene. It answers why you are doing the video, what your goal is, and how you will address or answer the problem or conflict. This is where you make an emotional connection with your visitors' needs and opinions.

You might present slides or charts of collected information. Statistics can help explain a solution or provide justification for your position. Keep slides very simple and vary them. Use charts, bar graphs, and pie charts. Comparison slides are also good.

However, stories are *always* better than diagrams or bar charts illustrating and analyzing statistics. Charts and numbers stimulate the mind but do nothing for the heart. Bullet points are bad for viewer retention. They don't convey a message of entertainment or fun. Think about TV how-to shows—like cooking. How many contain bullet points?

Authentic stories should inspire and persuade without being patronizing. Use emotions to convey energy and excitement and appeal to the heart. Identify some key events that propel your story forward. These might be good locations for *Calls to Action.*

Checklist for Your Story Concept

1. Make a storyboard. Using pen and paper, draw boxes of scene 1, 2, and so on with a short description of the message portrayed in each scene and what the viewer will see (props, person, etc.).

2. What is the goal of the video? Review your lists of *Calls to Action*. The video needs to tell the viewer what to do, why they should do it, and how they should do it. Visually portray a solution to the problem.

3. How can you make an emotional connection to increase your conversions? People reach for their wallets when they empathasize; feel similar or relate to the problem at hand. Your video story might share a personal journey or transition, or talk of overcoming an obstacle, a lesson learned, or perhaps a caution of some sort. Can the story connect with personal dreams of success and happiness?

4. Who, if anyone should be in the video? Who connects best with the audience's age, demographics, or interests?

5. How will you introduce yourself? This is optional, but if you do, on YouTube introductions are fairly casual.

6. State the problem or need you are solving. Does your story answer a journalist's questions:
   - Who, what, and when? - Concerning your product
   - Where? - Where is the service or product used?
   - Why? - Why is the price a valuable exchange for the product? This can be subtle, and it should help with conversions.
   - How? - How will your story create motivation to buy or sign up or accomplish the *Call to Action*.

7. Add your viewpoint. People want to know your thoughts; your opinion. Tell why you endorse or believe in the product, service, or solution.

8. Ask yourself: What will make this video shareable?

Script

After you have your storyboard, make a script. Changes made during scripting can save you hours of editing later. Scripting is also good practice for future outsourcing. If you are used to writing scripts, you will be prepared to eventually hand them to someone, and say, "I need a video for this."

The script is more than dialogue. The script is dialogue plus visual images. You might write dialogue on top of your storyboard or a page of dialogue with notes about visual images. As you write, ask yourself what images might go well with the dialogue. People come to video because they want to see something, so we need to give them action on the screen.

Stories are supposed to show and not tell. This is even more true when it comes to video. Look for dialogue that can be replaced with an image. This will also help make your video shorter.

Don't forget about energy. We often hear the camera adds ten pounds to our weight, but the camera also drains our energy. When writing the script, think about how you will keep your video full of energy, so viewers don't leave.

Start paying attention to TV commercials. Observe how fast the image changes in relation to the audio. Write down techniques you might use to appeal to your target audience.

Have a great title. Try to place your keywords in the front. Try browsing other videos or book covers for ideas on how to grab a viewer's attention.

Here are specific ideas and strategies for your script language:

- *Keywords:* Use them immediately in the beginning, once or twice in the middle (these might be long-tail versions), and again at the end.
- *About you:* "I'm author, founder, inventor, (etc.) of…"
- *Forecasting:* "I'm going to show you…" "I'm going to explain… but first, I want to ask you, tell you, show you… "
- *Educate:* "Here are some simple (lessons, etc.) on…"
- *Authentic:* "Because of my experience in…"
- *Honest:* "While I'm a novice at… I do know about..."
- *Vision:* "My (mission, goal, etc.) is…"
- *Promise:* "This video will show [# of] things you can do today to…"

- *Offer:* "If you [do this] I will personally (send you, give you, tell you, etc.)..."
- *Emotional Connections:* "Have you ever felt...," "Has this ever happened to you?" or "I can't stand it when..."
- *Emotional Change:* "What I learned from... that helped me was... "
- *Convince:* "Some fundamental points about... are..."
- *Solicit a Video Response:* "You can leave a video response on this page. We want to hear from you."
- *Sandwich approach:* Tell what you will cover, explain the issue at hand, and then summarize what you just said.

When you have a complete script. Let it sit for a day or so. Come back and try to cut the number of words in half. This helps you be as concise as you can, and eliminate any fluff. Viewers want a quality video providing value, in as little time as possible.

Read it out loud. Record yourself reading the script. Play it back. Can it stand on it's own, in case you want to turn it into a podcast? Does it sound like you? Is it a conversational, dinner table tone or too sales pitchy?

Read it pacing back and forth as if you were the head speaker at a conference. Is it natural? Don't hesitate to write "chuckle" or "pause" into your script to make it sound more natural. Include notes for when you should look directly into the camera. (Keep this simulated eye-to-eye contact short, just as you would when talking to a friend.)

Have someone else read your script and give you feedback.

If you decide to film yourself using a teleprompter, consider wearing sunglasses—no one will be able to tell you are reading. Ideally, limit your own time on camera in one location to 10-15 seconds, which equates to 2-3 sentences. Interrupt your speaking with images, slides, whiteboarding (an animated hand drawing an image), or animation. You might splice together several clips of you talking so you are first located on screen left and next, on screen right. This change of location diverts the viewers focus and helps maintain interest.

Playing a role may help you relax and sound conversational. Pretend you are a tour bus guide or a teacher in front of a classroom. You are the expert telling them about the solution. Add notes to your script to remind you to use your hands, hold the product, or make some gestures.

Embedded Video Check

Will you allow your video to be embedded? You should because this brings more views.

Give your script the embedded video check. Will it work as an embedded video? Make sure you didn't say, "Click the link in the description below." That won't work on someone else's website. You might say, "If you're watching this on YouTube, you can click below to..." or simply, "Visit my website at..."

Add *Calls to Action* in the script, along with notes for locations of branding banners or logos. This protects your work from users who may clip your video when embedding.

Screen Captures

Screen captures are instructional or tutorial videos that show you clicking around a computer screen to complete steps. Follow these script and procedure tips for a clean professional result:

1. Record the entire process with audio, including all the pauses and any mistakes.
2. Take the audio and type it out as a script.
3. Edit the script, cutting out any unnecessary dialogue.
4. Re-record the audio adding natural inflections.
5. Match the audio to the video in your favorite video editing software. You may have to clip the audio into segments or have to speed up portions of the screen capture so everything is aligned properly (in synch).

Audio Presentation Tips

Good audio is the *number one priority* in video creation. If the sound is poor, viewers will click away. Rehearse and record your script twice. The second recording always sounds more natural.

It's easier to match video to previously created audio, so after you have your script, create your audio first. Unless you are filming live, you can create your audio separately. Do this for screen capture, animation, whiteboarding, or slide presentations. (Download and use the free, user-friendly Audacity software found at: http://audacity.sourceforge.net/.)

Checklist for Your Video Presentation

1. *Have energy:* Laugh, smile, and try to imitate mannerisms used on TV. No monotone.

2. *Clap your hands on mistakes:* If you make a mistake recording audio, clap loudly. This sound will help to properly align video with audio during editing.

3. *Talk through the camera:* Pretend to talk to someone six feet in front of you, or behind the camera.

4. *Use casual conversational audio:* Pretend you are talking to a friend over coffee. Better yet, have a friend be there while you film and actually talk to this person.

5. *Tease and foreshadow:* Keep the viewer's attention and encourage them to keep watching. Say things like:
   - I'll have an offer for you at the end
   - This is step one of the three I will cover
6. *Add a wake-up call:* Bring drifting viewers back in.
   - Add a surprise prop or have a noise pop in
   - Say, "Remember you can hit pause to see this [chart]"
7. *Keywords:* Use your keywords several times in the audio, so they appear in the transcript and help with ranking.

8. *Make a verbal Call to Action:* Add your number one goal or objective to the audio.

9. *Include a social request:* In your audio, ask the viewer to share, like, subscribe, or comment.

10. *Do a "So What?" check:* When you think you are done, ask yourself why the viewer cares about this video and why he or she would share it to a friend?

Editing & Upload

Make interesting videos. Will your video include a person? On what type of background? Do you want to use a green screen to place the person on unique backgrounds? Will you add pop-up items within the video? How will you create your branding message? What music will you choose to set the tone?

To keep viewers attention when someone is talking, pop in an image overlay. This could be an object illustrating the concept (such as question marks for "idea" popping into a tutorial). You might also try an action or special effect illustrating a concept. You can find graphic sources in the back of this book.

You have roughly eight seconds to capture a viewers attention. For most videos, you should open with exactly what you bring to the table. Tell the viewer what they will see today; follow with your five second branding, and begin the information.

An exception is when creating a video ad (such as for AdWords). In this case, you might open with your branding, because even if the viewer clicks to skip the ad, they have seen your logo or website URL and heard your *Call to Action*.

Edit out extra breathing, unnatural pauses, and background sound. Was a fire engine passing by?

Close your video with as much visual *Call to Action* possible. This might mean showing an order form or a screen shot of the page they will land on when they click through or what they will see to download your free offer given for subscribing.

Use your software to end your video with three boxes in a row with thumbnail images of readable text that could apply to any of your videos (such as: Favorite Video, Next Video, and More on this topic). After uploading, you can add annotation links to these images, and because they are generic text images, you can update the links as needed to promote new videos and increase views.

Create an awesome custom thumbnail image. Be careful with the lower right corner, because YouTube places the time length of your video there and you don't want your logo or words cut off.

Check for user retention. Does your viewer need to watch to the end to see how it will end? Is it viewable on a small screen like a cell phone? Play your video to someone else for feedback. Watch the video without sound. Listen to the video without viewing the footage. Is it clear? This means it's also podcast ready. Covered everything? Then, it's time to upload and optimize (*See* p. 48).

Monetize

We've really been discussing monetization all along. We've been talking strategies to connect your viewer to your product or service. All these strategies will help your video rank higher in search results, which means you will be found and have the opportunity to make a sales conversion.

You might notice that we've not addressed viral marketing. We've discussed connecting to leaders in your niche which may assist in something going viral, but for the most part, our focus has been on consistent *evergreen* targeted traffic. When we hear the term viral, it is usually, "That video went viral." Notice the past tense. Going viral is valuable, but it does not create long term evergreen sales conversions.

Along with targeted traffic, there are two more ways to earn money from videos. The first is to use Google's AdSense program. Here you receive a commission from permitting other companies to place ads on your video. The second is Affiliate Marketing where you receive a commission from selling another company's product or service. We've demonstrated use of a few affiliate links throughout this book.

AdSense on YouTube

In setting up your channel, you should have activated monetization which allows you to permit ads on your video. When you're focused on your own business profit, you might choose to only monetize a few videos. This is because every time someone clicks on an ad, they are taken away from your *Call to Action*. This means you lost your opportunity to connect with the viewer. In most cases, it doesn't make sense to give up your own connection for the income you might receive from AdSense. AdSense can also decrease your retention rate and thus, lower your rankings.

That being said, some people are very successful at using AdSense. These people usually have significant traffic, receive high paying ads, and their business goal is solely to *earn income through advertising*. To learn more about AdSense search the Internet for AdSense forums and articles.

Affiliate Marketers

Promoting affiliate products is difficult with video. You need to have trust with the audience and come from a very neutral unbiased position. Your honest reviews should include what you don't like and what can be improved. Reviews should also be relevant to your audience. You might need to spend more time identifying your "buying" audience to be successful.

As an affiliate marketer, you will want to check the fine print of your affiliate terms before you create a product video. Some companies may not permit you to create a video, or they may permit you to create a video, but not to upload it to YouTube. You would have to host it elsewhere. You should be careful not to destroy your affiliate relationship or have your affiliate account shut down, just because you created a video.

Where should you place affiliate links?

Affiliate links can be placed in the YouTube description, or you link to your website URL and place your affiliate link there, on the landing page. When deciding where to send a viewer, consider:

- *Best for Viewer:* The best path for your viewer is the shortest path to what the *viewer wants*. In most cases, this would be a direct link to the product or service.
- *Best for Ranking and Tracking*: Every link from YouTube is an inbound link, so you might choose to link to your website page. Just make sure your website has *additional* valuable information for the viewer. Then on your website page, link to your affiliate product.

Test both methods over a period of time and over special occasions like holidays, to see which method pulls the best, desired conversions for your business.

As an affiliate, remember to take advantage of embedding videos created by others. You can embed someone else's camera review into your blog article and place your affiliate link below the video. This saves you time and you could potentially take home commissions for a video review you did nothing to create.

Paid Channel Subscriptions

In May 2013, YouTube launched the paid channels. Visit http://www.YouTube.com/channels/paid_channels to get a feel for how people are using paid channels.

Because this is a new feature, we have yet to see the impact on businesses. Several questions come to mind:

1. Will paid channels rank higher than free in search results?

2. Will your subscriber levels drop if you begin charging to view your videos?

3. How much should you charge subscribers?

4. Will your subscriber levels *increase* as users decide *not* to pay for the channels that do begin charging a fee? Maybe you will pick up some new subscribers looking for a free source.

5. If a charging a fee reduces your subscriber level, how much would you need to charge to achieve your desired income? For example. if your channel was bringing in $1,000 a month and you have 2,000 subscribers. You could charge $2 per month and drop down to 500 subscribers with no change in income. (500 × $2 = $1,000)

Stealth Webinars

You've probably heard of webinars, the live events where you can watch a presentation. These webinars can actually be Stealth Webinars (meaning they are pre-recorded) but appear to be live.

This is another venue for your videos. Software can help you prerecord a video and run it as a webinar when you are not actually there. You might add this webinar to a sequence of emails directing your customer down a buying path. Have the third email of the sequence contain a link that says, "Watch our upcoming Webinar, sign up here."

(This goes beyond using YouTube and the scope of this book, but you can find useful information online.)

Video Calls (Hangouts on Air - Live View)

Hangout

In setup, you opened a Google+ account. This permits you to participate in streaming live video chats (also known as Video Calls, Hangouts on Air, or YouTube Live View). Video Calls are like webinars, except you see participants in a live video feed. You should have a web camera and earphones for best results.

Our focus is on the *Live Hangout on Air* of up to 10 participants; broadcast to up to 100 viewers. (You can use a private hangout for private chats, such as with family or close friends.)

When a live hangout is completed, the person who began the hangout can save the entire footage as a video on his or her channel. This concept has huge potential.

We want to be able to hold a Live Video Call using our ***Google+ Page*** and upon completion, have it automatically post to our ***YouTube business channel,*** and have that automatically feed into social media. That's a system.

CAUTION:

As you begin exploring connecting YouTube and your Google+ Page, read and re-read any Google tutorials. If you ever see a *delete* button, be very careful. Better yet, DON'T CLICK. There have been numerous cases of people thinking they were deleting a Google+ Page and **they deleted (closed) their entire YouTube channel!** This happened even when the text on the screen only referred to the Google+ Page. Evidently the culprit is in how the Google+ Page is connected to YouTube. (Hopefully it will become more user friendly.) The YouTube to Google+ Pages connection is in Beta Testing (as of Spring 2013). Expect some issues and be very careful.

(We will post some links to read about this issue at: http://www.KidsandMoneyToday.com/video-resources/)

Why hold Video Calls/Hangouts?

1. *Free Traffic:* Hangouts are another traffic generator and opportunity for subscriptions (with the potential to reach 100 viewers per broadcast). And it's free!

2. *Another Video:* When your hangout is complete, it becomes yet another video for you to collect views, attract new subscribers, or even convert customers (assuming you have a *Call to Action* in the hangout). They can help grow your brand and add additional income.

3. *Fast Video Creation:* You don't need a fancy camera to create the video, only a web camera. You skip the editing phase. No worries about clipping, special effects, or technical issues (like frames per second, rendering, or the file formats of Mp4, .MOV, .AVI and .WMV). Your video can post immediately to YouTube and to social media sites (if your defaults and automatic posting are set).

4. *Fast Enhancement:* In YouTube, use the Enhancement tool in your video editor to change things like the lighting, color, or blur all faces. (Enhancement maintains your original footage, views, likes, and comments.)

5. *Edit and Create New Videos:* In the YouTube Editor, you can insert photos, audio, transitions, other video clips, and more. This is great for those wishing to forgo purchasing video creation software. (Editing creates a new video listing URL that can be ranked and added to playlists. You may wish to keep the original for its views.)

6. *Quotes and Testimonials:* Use YouTube's video editor to extract clips and quotations from Hangouts to use in your next video, or Live Call. You might also capture a Hangout when you are with a customer who has just praised your product or service. Say, "Thanks so much. Would you mind giving me a quote on video?" Use your phone to quickly set up a Hangout. With only a few clicks, you can add a testimonial to your channel.

7. *Picture Capture:* Capture a picture from within the Hangout to use as a thumbnail or for social sharing.

8. *Viewers love Live:* YouTube users like visual, and *live visual* should be even better. Who wants to watch a football game the next day—instead of watching it live?

9. *Branding:* Live Calls allow your customer to see you. This can help with branding (build trust and loyalty). Your business is a little more real; a little more personable.

10. *Social Exposure and Connection:* Video Calls are aimed at connecting socially. Google wants you to easily click on your phone and see the person you want to talk to. They're supposed to be fun—thus the name "Hangout."

11. *Niche Exposure:* Use this as another way to connect with niche leaders. Invite them to do an interview with you.

12. *Screen Share + Free Screen Capture:* With Video Calls, you can screen share. This means you can open up software on your own device, give a tutorial, and everyone can see it. Plus, it's being recorded for you. (No need to purchase a screen recording software.)

13. *Sales Opportunity:* Embed a Hangout onto your website and invite people to watch at that URL. Promote the URL to subscribers as: "View Us Live Every Tuesday." Add the URL to emails, newsletters, and website pages, and surround the webpage with your *Calls to Action*, affiliate links, and seasonal sales. (Update the page with the code of each new Hangout before you go live.)

   - You cannot create clickable links in a Live Call, but you can display or say aloud a URL that your viewer could type in their own browser. After the broadcast, you can use annotations to add clickable links to the video.

14. *Google Search Ranking Boost:* At the moment, Live Call videos are usually ranking above other videos.

15. *Ranking Opportunity:* Hangouts offer another opportunity to dominate Google Search results for a given keyword. Your domain (article or home page) could rank in position number one, your hangout in position two, and

your playlist in position three. Even with small shifts of results, you could own three out of the top ten positions.

16. *Google+ Search Benefits:* Google+ is also a search engine and it gives better results than searching on other social media sites. You can be in the first position, especially if users use a filter to restrict their results only to Hangouts.

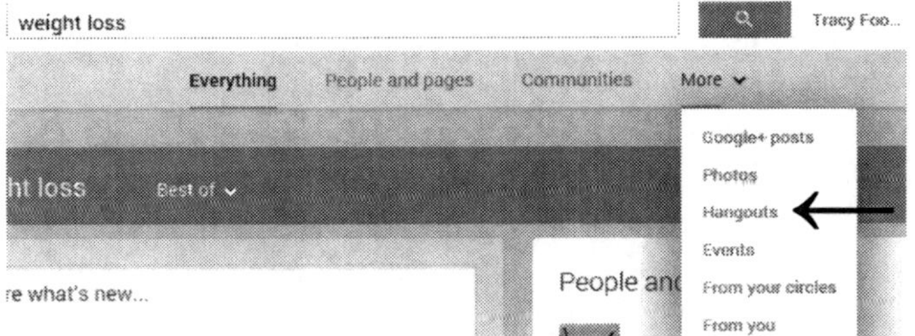

17. *Rich Snippets:* The Live Call turns into a YouTube video that will display attractively in Google Search Results with a thumbnail image. Even if you are position three or four, you might pull in more clicks than position one.

18. *Age Benefits:* This is new and if you begin now, you will have the "age" benefit over those who learn about it later.

19. *Automatic Analytic Tracking:* After the video posts to YouTube, analytics tracks all views and stats, just as with any other video.

20. *Connect with Google:* Google Search results, Google+ (where Live Calls take place), and YouTube are all owned by Google. One would expect better rankings by participating in all three.

What's not to love?

This is a growing feature. This means dropped connections, loss of audio, and other technical difficulties do arise. You may not want to do a hangout for a large important business event.

Live Calls are not really evergreen marketing. They are live events, which means they will take your time. This is something to consider as your business grows. Do you want to be doing Hangouts in five or ten years? How often?

Video Ads

AdWords

You can begin to create video ads either within your YouTube account or directly from your AdWords account. If you followed our channel set-up steps, you should have already signed up for AdWords and already be tracking potential remarketing lists.

Video advertising will not only bring you some business conversions, but it brings you additional views. This helps rank your videos on YouTube and Google Search results.

In YouTube, go to *Video Manager* > *Upload* and choose the video you want to use as an ad. Click *Edit* and choose *Promote* from the dropdown menu. Follow the steps to create your campaign.

Sample screen shot

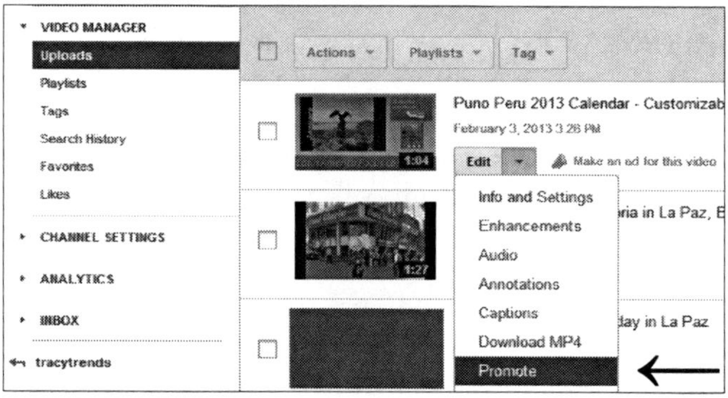

Using AdWords, you can bid on different keywords and your reports will tell you the average position of your video ad, click through rate, and cost for each keyword. Use your emotional and transformation (change) words in your ads to connect with viewers and obtain higher conversions. Your should test, evaluate, and edit your promotion to maximize your performance.

True View Ads

True View ads are campaigns where you only pay if the viewer chooses to click on your ad. There are four types:

- TrueView In-stream: Your ad will appear as a preview before another video.
- TrueView In-slate: Your ad is shown before YouTube partner videos that are 10 minutes or longer.
- TrueView In-search: Your ad appears in search results.
- TrueView In-display: Your ad appears to the right of a video that users are watching.

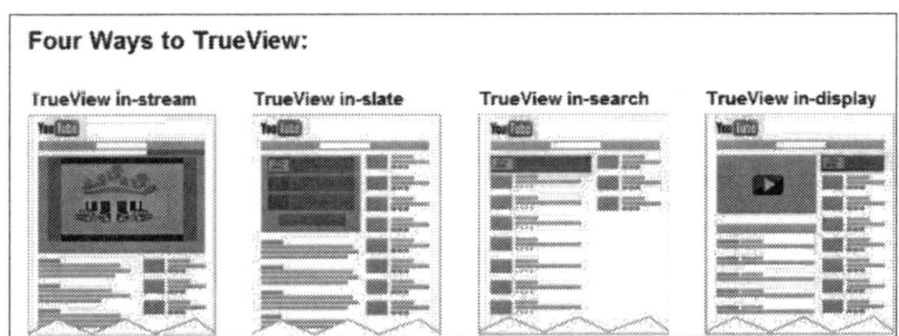

For more information search YouTube Help for *TrueView,* or visit http://www.YouTube.com/yt/advertise/trueview.html.

It takes some time to learn how to run a successful AdWords campaign. Our purpose here is to introduce using AdWords video in your business marketing.

Creating and writing ads that will rank in the first position shown to Internet users is an entirely different algorithm. It includes unique things like the quality of your landing page (the page your ad brings the visitor to), how much you are willing to pay, and what your competitors are bidding.

Since it's so easy to build your remarketing lists, AdWords is definitely worth exploring. (If you can market to someone who has watched your videos, they are already at some location in your sales funnel.)

Look for AdWords tutorials and online forums to learn more. The best book we've found is: *Advanced Google AdWords* by Brad Geddes found at our affiliate link: http://www.amazon.com/exec/obidos/ASIN/B007RSUSKA/tracytrends.

Call to Action Overlay

When you have connected your AdWords account to YouTube *and* created a TrueView ad, you should have an *additional tab* in your YouTube video editor titled *Call to Action Overlay*.

To run the overlay ad, you complete the boxes shown in the image below:

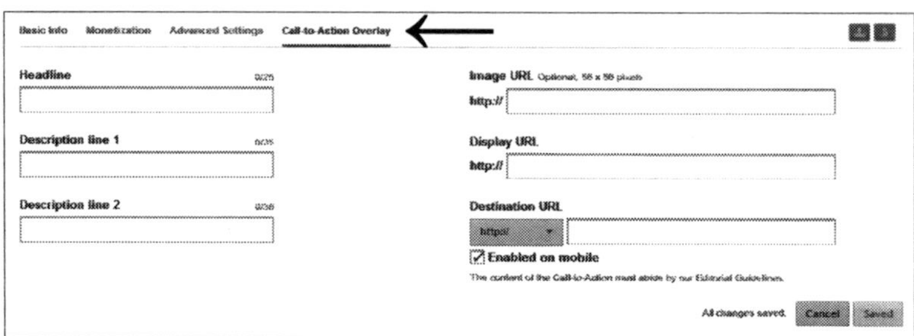

For the duration of your AdWords campaign, you will have this option to run overlay ads on videos across YouTube (not just on your own channel).

As soon as a video begins to play, the overlay appears as a link in a rectangle shape on the lower part of a video. The viewer can choose to close it, if so desired.

You specify the destination link for the *Call to Action Overlay* at no additional charge. This is another way to take advantage of your AdWords campaigns within YouTube.

Visit YouTube Help at http://support.Google.com/YouTube and search for *About Call-to-Action Overlays* to find an article explaining more.

Facebook Ads

As mentioned, increasing views plays a role in the ranking of your video. Another way to increase views, as well as conversions, for your business is to use Facebook ads.

Facebook ads can also be targeted, similar to the remarketing strategies already mentioned.

In the case of Facebook ads, you might target your competitor's followers. Use *Fan Page Promoted Posts* which allow you to target friends-of-friends or people who liked your competitors Facebook Page. You're targeting ads based on user interactions, in this case, they clicked like on your competitor's page. If they like your competitor, they may like your product too. This approach might produce very successful conversions for your business.

A common question with video ads is whether to use an actual video in your Facebook ad or an image. You should test both options because what works for one niche, may not work for another. But, don't be hesitant to use the video itself. Include a link below the video to allow viewers to click through to your website. Often people will watch the video on Facebook and still click through to learn more.

If you are interested in Facebook, look for forums and leaders on Facebook who have expertise in advertising with video.

Quick Summary Checklists

Your Business Channel

1. Create your channel URL with a business name or keywords.

2. Upload your banner image and profile icon

3. Set your Privacy settings.

4. Completely fill out your *About Page*
    - Channel Description
    - Custom Links (first link shows in your header)
    - Social Links (first four links show in your header)
    - Featured channels
    - Subscriptions (choose public or private)

5. Complete everything in *Account Settings* with special attention to:
    - Connected Accounts: Set up automatic activity posting (as desired) to FB or Twitter for uploads, likes, comments, and playlists
    - Privacy: Choose to keep likes and/or subscriptions private

6. Set your preferences in *My Subscriptions* (Group your subscriptions as collections and set your notifications.)

7. Set your preferences for default video uploads.

8. Change your country.

9. Enable monetization and connect your AdSense Account.

10. Verify your Associated Website.

11. Verify your Account Status / Become a Verified Partner

12. Create a Google Analytics Property ID for your business website at http://www.Google.com/analytics.

13. Create a Google Analytics Property ID for your YouTube channel.

14. Create a Google AdWords account and link your YouTube account to Google AdWords. Do this by visiting: http://AdWords.google.com/

15. Begin collecting Remarking lists (Choose which YouTube visitors you wish to add to your advertising lists.)

16. Join Google+ social network.

17. Review your Account Status for full activation and authorization of YouTube features.

YouTube Quick Start

1. Create playlists.

2. Embed playlists and other people's videos on your website with:

   - links to subscribe to your YouTube channel.
   - links to subscribe to your blog or newsletter

YouTube Community

1. Subscribe to leaders in your niche.

2. Comment on videos in your niche and respond to comments on your own channel.

3. Check and respond to your inbox.

4. Create Playlists.

5. Embed related niche videos on your business website with a link to subscribe to *your own* YouTube channel.

Video Marketing Plan

Summary:

- Determine your goals.
- Know your audience.
- Write content (create videos) for this audience.
- Rank well for this audience and they will convert.

Detailed:

1. Make a list of your goals and objectives. Include a calendar schedule, such as your plan during holidays.

2. Create your *Calls to Action* to achieve these goals.

3. Identify your target audience and what they want from an emotional perspective. (*See* p. 33)

4. Research niche leaders and subscribe to new channels.

5. Understand the stages in your sales funnel.

6. Participate in the YouTube community. Subscribe, comment and share videos within your niche.

7. Research the keywords your audience uses to find their solutions. (*See* p. 45)

8. Make a plan to bring viewers to a desired state (buying, subscribing, downloading, and so on).

9. Choose where you will post your videos for exposure; where you want viewers to watch your videos. (*See* ideas to increase views p. 59, comments p. 64, subscribers p. 66)

10. Optimize your videos to rank in the top positions for your keywords on search engines and YouTube.

11. Make a prediction for the outcome of each video uploaded.

12. Decide how you will measure the success of each video.

Video Optimization & Marketing

1. Create your *Title, Description,* and *Tags* using your keywords.

2. Upload your custom Thumbnail image or choose one from those suggested by YouTube.

3. Add your *Calls to Action* in Annotations.

4. Download, edit, and re-upload your Transcript.

5. Choose whether to activate Monetization for this video.

6. Add this video to a current Playlist or make a new one.

7. Embed your video in an article on your website with a text link directly below, linking its YouTube URL.

8. Share to social media from YouTube, your website, and on the social media sites. (Use scheduling if it's available)

9. Subscribe to another channel in the same niche as your video.

10. Repurpose your video for any of these marketing ideas:
    - Embedded on a guest blog
    - Newsletter
    - Reviews
    - Podcasts
    - PDF
    - RSS feeds
    - DVD
    - Webinar
    - Hangout presentation
    - Thank you note

11. Consider running a Video AdWords or Facebook campaign, and evaluate it, modify, and run again

12. Repeat for each video

Repeatable Video System

1. Prioritize your video ideas (*See* p. 88) based on analytical data.

2. Apply all the concepts from your *Video Marketing Plan Checklist*: What is the goal, the *Call to Action*, etc.

3. Sketch your story: A storyboard of each scene (*See* p. 91)

4. Write and edit your script (*See* p. 92 & 98): Detailed text along with gestures, *Call to Action* verbiage and images, etc.

5. Does the script pass the embedded video check?

6. What makes the video shareable?

7. Audio: Record and edit your audio using keywords.

8. Film: Create your video footage with a camera or Power Point, animation or screen capture software. (This might be done together with the audio step, if you plan for a person to talk.)

9. Edit: Finalize your video using your favorite software. Include keywords and a visual and audio *Call to Action*.

10. Create Images: Make a custom thumbnail, a 200x200 image for your website, and any other sizes needed for your plan for social media posting.

11. Schedule: Upload your video and schedule it to post according to your plan for consistent uploading.

12. Complete all the steps in the *Video Optimization & Marketing* checklist.

13. Monitor your rankings and conversions using software and analytics. Evaluate and adjust as needed.

14. Repeat: Review this checklist again for each video. Batch process in small groups.

Analytics Questions

1. How well are your videos ranking for their primary keyword or phrase? On YouTube? On Google Search?

2. How well are your videos ranking on YouTube and Google Search for secondary and long-tail keywords?

3. Are you adjusting your titles, descriptions, and tags to take advantage of popular topics and daily trends?

4. Can you do more to increase your video views?

5. Where are your videos being watched and embedded? Are you creating more videos targeted at this audience and sharing them on a regular basis?

6. Are you observing keywords that your users have entered and creating new videos for these?

7. Are you monitoring your users interaction with your annotations and making adjustments?

8. Are you evaluating where your videos are shared?

9. Can you make more videos similar to those that pull in the most subscribers?

10. Are you watching retention rate and using it to predict the best types of new videos to create for your audience?

11. How well do you maintain your audience attention?

12. Is anyone clicking your YouTube Description links? Which ones and on what type of video?

13. Which social networks or external sites send your website the most visits?

14. Which social networks send the most conversions?

15. Which social media sites send the most engaging customers (based on time on site and pages viewed)?

Resources

The following resources (free and paid) may assist you with your video marketing strategies. Please read all terms of use. To view this list as links please visit:

http://www.KidsandMoneyToday.com/video-resources/

URL Quick List

These are important URLs listed throughout the book. Remember to change the name references to your own channel name, where applicable.

Rank Tracker Software:
http://www.kidsandmoneytoday.com/rank-checker/

URL Shortener, Cloaker, and Tracker (Paid):
http://www.kidsandmoneytoday.com/track-link

WordPress Rank Tracker Plugin:
http://www.kidsandmoneytoday.com/video-rank.

YouTube Opt-in *confirmation* link:
http://YouTube.com/subscription_center?add_user=*UserName*

YouTube activity (See someone's):
http://www.YouTube.com/user/*username*/feed.

Animation

- http://www.kidsandmoneytoday.com/animation (our affiliate link)

Apps

- *FiLMmic Pro App: (*Best Video App of 2011)
- iMovie Video Editing App for iPad

Audio

- http://audiojungle.net/
- http://audacity.sourceforge.net/
- http://incompetech.com/
- http://www.premiumbeat.com
- http://www.shockwave-sound.com
- http://triplescoopmusic.com
- http://www.yakitome.com/tts/text_to_speech

CD & DVD

- http://www.createspace.com/Products/DVD/
- http://www.cdbaby.com/
- http://www.kunaki.com/

Education - Online

- http://en.wikipedia.org/wiki/YouTube
- http://www.YouTube.com/yt/playbook/
- http://www.YouTube.com/videomaker
- http://www.videomaker.com/YouTube

Education (Printed Materials)

- http://www.videomaker.com/magazine/

Equipment

- iPhone audio adapters at:
http://www.kvconnection.com/Default.asp
- iPhone mount at:
http://blog.fastcap.com/2013/magnetic-iphone-mount/
- Shotgun Microphone at (our affiliate link)
http://www.amazon.com/exec/obidos/ASIN/B008S0YJCE/tracytrends
- Snagit at (our affiliate link)
http://www.amazon.com/exec/obidos/ASIN/B007H083NC/tracytrends
- Web Camera:
http://www.amazon.com/exec/obidos/ASIN/B006JH8T3S/tracytrends
- Wireless microphone: at (our affiliate link)
http://www.amazon.com/exec/obidos/ASIN/B001E104D2/tracytrends
- Velcro Tripod: attach Velcro to your iPhone and any wall or surface in order to create an instant tripod (affiliate link)
http://www.amazon.com/exec/obidos/ASIN/B001O6T2ZS/tracytrends

Graphics

- http://cooltext.com/
- http://creativecommons.org/
- http://www.iconfinder.com/
- http://openclipart.org/
- http://www.presentermedia.com/
- http://us.fotolia.com/

Landing Pages

- http://www.kidsandmoneytoday.com/landing-pages/ (our affiliate link to templates we use for landing pages)

Monetizing

- http://coull.com/
- http:// www.google.com/AdSense/

Opt-in List Building Video Player

- http://www.kidsandmoneytoday.com/video-player

Organizing Your Schedule

- http://trello.com/
- http://www.actionenforcer.com/online/
(free online version of ActionEnforcer)
- http://www.actionxpert.com/
(paid software download of ActionEnforcer)

Outsourcing

- http://fiverr.com/
- http://www.odesk.com/
- http://www.taskrabbit.com/

PodCast Help

- http://www.libsyn.com/
- http://www.podbean.com/
- http://www.scribd.com/
- http://WordPress.org/plugins/podpress/

Rank Checking

- http://www.kidsandmoneytoday.com/video-rank
(our affiliate link to a WordPress Plugin)
- http://www.kidsandmoneytoday.com/rank-checker/
(our affiliate link to rank checking software)

Social Media Sharing & Scheduling Your Posts

- DoShare Chrome Add-on (Google this to install)
- http://bufferapp.com/
- http://www.kidsandmoneytoday.com/auto-schedule
(our affiliate link to auto-schedule software - free trial)
- http://ifttt.com/

Teleprompter

- OnAir App from iTunes

Video Creation

- http://www.animoto.com
- http://www.flixpress.com/
- http://www.fotomagico.com/
- http://www.onetruemedia.com/
- http://www.pond5.com/
- http://snapguide.com/
- http://videohive.net/

Video Distribution

- http://www.easywebvideo.com/
- http://heyspread.com/
- http://www.oneload.com/
- http://www.trafficgeyser.com/
- http://www.tubemogul.com/
- http://www.kidsandmoneytoday.com/social-player (our affiliate link to a player with social media links)
- http://wistia.com/

WordPress Plugins

- http://www.kidsandmoneytoday.com/video-player (our affiliate link to LeadPlayer)
- http://onepress-media.com/plugin/tweet-2-unlock-for-twitter-WordPress
- http://www.popupdomination.com/live/
- http://WordPress.org/plugins/share-this/
- http://WordPress.org/plugins/gplus-comments/
- http://www.kidsandmoneytoday.com/track-link (our affiliate link to a URL shortener, tracker, and cloaker)
- http://www.kidsandmoneytoday.com/video-rank (our affiliate link to a rank checker WordPress Plugin)

Index

Space for Your Own Notes

Easily Order this Book

- at your local bookstore
- from the publisher at www.tracytrends.com
- online from Amazon at affiliate link:

www.amazon.com/exec/obidos/ASIN/098147375X/tracytrends

Review Request

If you would recommend this book to others, please consider writing a 5 star review on Amazon.com.

How to write a review in four easy steps:

1. On the Internet visit http://www.amazon.com
2. Enter 0-9814737-5-X in the search box on Amazon
3. About half way down, click *Create Your Own Review*
4. Please tell others what you liked about this book

Reader Comments and Inquiries

Comments, inquiries, or documented updates should be emailed to kidsandmoneytoday@gmail.com. All remarks are considered for future editions and/or the website to further assist readers.

To view updates not included in this printing, visit:
http://www.kidsandmoneytoday.com/video-updates/

Comment on online marketing at:
http://www.KidsandMoneyToday.com
or connect on social networks

CPSIA information can be obtained at www.ICGtesting.com
Printed in the USA
LVOW12s1517180615

442981LV00002B/455/P

9 780981 473758